Advance Praise for
LOST, KIDNAPPED, EATEN ALIVE!

This wonderful story of human endurance and per-severance in Croatia is **masterfully told**. In only a few pages, King acquaints us with her heroine, with a culture, a national history and the age-old technique of harvesting silk from silkworms. The author's touch is light and endearing, and **her story stays with you**...."

—Society of American Travel Writers judges about
  "Silk from Ashes," which earned the 2013
  Lowell Thomas Gold Award for Cultural Tourism

Whether she's working to help save lemurs in Madagascar or communing with a one-legged toucan in Costa Rica, King brings **uncommon heart and soul** to her travel stories. And she's always on the lookout for adventure .... From start to finish, *Lost, Kidnapped, Eaten Alive* is a **rollicking ride.**

—Michael Shapiro
  Author, *A Sense of Place: Great Travel Writers
  Talk About Their Craft, Lives, and Inspiration*

If I were going to be eaten alive (or lost, or kidnapped), I'd prefer it was in the company of Laurie McAndish King. I'd be **laughing out loud** as the anaconda swallowed me—and **learning fascinating facts** about its digestive process, and the global distribution of pythons.

—Jeff Greenwald
  Author, *Shopping for Buddhas* and
  The Size of the World

What are the two things I adore about every one of the stories in *Lost, Kidnapped, Eaten Alive*? The **compassion** and the **wit**. King made me want to protect a toucan named Stravinsky, laugh at French lingerie (not to mention French appliances), and savor mussels in Apulia. Each story is an adventure, but each **traces the geography of the heart as well as that of the world.**

—Constance Hale
   Travel writer and author of *Sin and Syntax* and
   Vex, Hex, Smash, Smooch

When travelers comment about how the road teaches them things they couldn't learn any other way, they are usually referring to the pitfalls and scourges that can confront us. But King reminds us in her **delightful** new collection of travel tales that there is another way to hit the road—and that way is … **spirited with surprise**."

—Phil Cousineau
   Author, *The Art of Pilgrimage and The Book of Roads*

King's book is a traveler's guide to the planet. Whether she is encountering Africa's big cats or Madagascar's lemurs, becoming one with the Australian rainforest or learning about silkworm smuggling in Croatia, she **transports readers to faraway places with vivid details** of cultural quirks, real people, flora, fauna, and food.

—Camille Cusumano
   Author, *Tango, an Argentine Love Story*

King's great gift is her **ability to transport her readers** to wherever she happens to be, and to share her experience. While she's tracking lemurs through Madagascar's rain forests, for instance, we viscerally feel the pulsing...humidity of the leech-infested environment, even as we become deeply concerned about the plight of those charismatic yet fragile remote human relatives.

—Dr. Ian Tattersall
　Author, *Masters of the Planet: The Search for Our Human Origins*
　Curator Emeritus, Division of Anthropology
　American Museum of Natural History

———•—

Whether encircled by angry, spear-waving Maasai warriors, fording leech-filled streams or stranded in the blistering Australian Outback, King's **sharp intelligence, impish humor,** and adventurous spirit are on brilliant display in this wonderful collection of travel essays. **I couldn't put it down!**

—Suzanne Rodriguez
　Author, *Found Meals of the Lost Generation* and *Wild Heart: A Life—Natalie Clifford Barney and the Decadence of Literary Paris*

———•—

King's description of eating figs in southern Italy is **luscious**. I included an excerpt from her moment of "gustatory ecstasy" in my book on writing as an example of **succulence**.

—Laura Deutsch
　Author, *Writing from the Senses*

When it comes to adventure travel, King is a gourmand who leaves nothing off the table. Some-times the diner—Italian horse steak, Balinese luwak-ingested coffee beans—sometimes the dinner—think hungry lions, crazed mosquitoes, leeches—she serves up a **delicious feast for the curious mind.**

With insight and a ready wit, Laurie takes you with her to **hidden worlds** of women—an erotic Celtic goddess, a pricey French underwear boutique, Croatian women who hide silk-worm eggs in their bras—and survives close encounters as Tunisian men try to kidnap her, and a Kenyan Maasai initiates a sudden wedding.

Along with excitement Laurie slows to offer **moving meditations,** reflecting on nature, life, and travels with her father. And just when you think she's surely ready for the easy chair and a nice travel book, she serves up another delicious tale *con gusto*.

—Joanna Biggar
  Author, *That Paris Year*
  Member, The Society of Women Geographers

What a fabulous book! I didn't know whether to buckle my seat belt or book a flight to the far wilds of the planet as I turned the pages of *Lost, Kidnapped, Eaten Alive*, well into the night. King takes readers deep into the traveller's soul in these intimate, frightening, endearing stories. They **so thoroughly deliver the unique sense of each locale, readers should qualify for a special passport stamp** upon completion!

—Suzanna Stinnett
  Author, *Little Shifts* and *The Sugar Divorce*

In this collection of short travel stories—part natural wonder, part cultural tour—King puts a new spin on globe-trotting through her **lively and intimate vignettes**. From what makes a Parisian woman "Parisian" (hint: see lingerie), to what makes a Maasai man tick, the dizzying array of snapshots reads **like a close friend's postcards-turned-keepsakes**. A suspenseful and joyous romp around the world!

—Tressa Berman, Ph.D.
  Anthropologist and author

I love Laurie's eco-biology pieces. She had me at the opening of an early story: "The first time I tracked lions..." The *first* time? Here's a woman who takes the term **adventure travel** seriously! Talk about armchair travel. **This is a very fun trip**.

—Pamela Feinsilber
  Editor; culture critic; former travel editor,
  San Francisco magazine

King's stories immediately draw you into her adventures. Her **keen insight** and evocative nature resonate right off the pages and dare you to take part in her journeys. My personal favorite is Laurie's search for "Sheela-na-Gig" in Country Cork, Ireland — **a provocative tale** of the "fertile darkness."

—Molly Blaisdell
  Author, *Her Journey to 50*

Memories are what we hope to treasure from our travels, but who needs the perfect holiday? King shows how to turn a **strange, scary, funny, wild** and crazy moment in time into a **life-altering adventure** to remember.

—Judy Salamancha
Director, Central Coast Writers Conference
Author, *Colonel Baker's Field: An American Pioneer Story*

———•———

King is a **savvy, smart, and humorous** traveling companion, for she does not merely write stories, she invites us along as she inquires, investigates, and **digs deep into the histories, cultures, cuisines** and characters of places all over the world… be ready for a **wild ride.**

—Erin Byrne
Editor, *Vignettes & Postcards*

———•———

Insightful and humorous, Laurie McAndish King's richly varied travel stories are full of the ingredients any successful travel writer needs — **passion, perception and surprise**. And yes, she can eat a horse!"

—Connie Burke
Editor, *Venturing in Ireland: Quest for the Modern Celtic Soul* and *Venturing in Italy: Puglia, Land between Two Seas*

I still smile—months after reading *Lost, Kidnapped, Eaten Alive*—as I recall its hilarious stories from the far corners of the earth. You are bound to savor … King's **quirky world view**.

—Tom Wilmer
  Author, *The Wine Seeker's Guide to Livermore Valley* and *Romancing the Coast: Romantic Getaways Along the California Coast*
  Host, NPR Affiliate Radio Travel Show

———•·•———

This book doesn't merely contain tasty stories; King's **curiosity always takes her deeper** — whether she's explaining why Apulians call fried bread cubes "husband-blinders," discovering how an odd Balinese critter is key to producing the world's most coveted coffee, or revealing that yeast is asexual (who knew?).

—Gayle Keck
  Travel & food writer; proprietor of FoodTourFinder.com

———•·•———

If the only story you read is about being stalked by lions in the Okavango Delta, *Lost, Kidnapped, Eaten Alive* is worth the price of admission. Laurie's writing is so **fresh and fun**, I kept smiling all the way through this delightful collection of misfired adventures….**a treasure**.

—Linda Ballou
  Author, *Lost Angel Walkabout—One Traveler's Tales*

Laurie McAndish King's **droll, delightful and insightful observations** from her far flung journeys are a terrific companion for armchair travel, taking readers (and our brains) to adventures where most of us have never gone before.

—Judith Horstman
    Author, *The Scientific American Healthy Aging Brain*

For those who remember the **wild, funny** and very well-written article about lemur volunteering in Madagascar by travel writer Laurie McAndish King that appeared in one of my books, King has a new book out full of more fab travel stories. **Can't wait to get mine!**

—Nola Lee Kelsey
    Author, *Animal Addict's Guide to Global Volunteer Travel*

Some of my favorite travel stories are in this collection. Whether she is tracking down the perfect French kiss in Paris, making friends with the animals in Costa Rica, or coming up with a new trinity in Ireland, King never fails to "bring it" to the page.

—Linda Watanabe McFerrin
    Author of *Namako, The Hand of Buddha* and *Dead Love*

LOST KIDNAPPED EATEN ALIVE!

TRUE STORIES FROM A
CURIOUS TRAVELER

LOST KIDNAPPED EATEN ALIVE!

LAURIE MCANDISH KING

Destination Insights
www.destinationinsights.com

In the interest of privacy, I changed the names and identifying details of many of the people I met or traveled with, and some of the places I visited.

Interior photos:
Solar eclipse, page 208 by Kubotake (Wikimedia Commons).
Compass, page xxii; Stravinsky, page 18; Bali Face, page 138; Camel in Outback, page 174; Crossroads, page 190; Mountain, page 246 © 2014 JM Shubin.

All other photos © 2014 Laurie McAndish King.
Published by:
Destination Insights
www.destinationinsights.com

Cover design, interior design by JM Shubin, Shubin Design (www.shubindesign.com).

CATALOGING IN PUBLICATION DATA:
Lost, Kidnapped, Eaten Alive: True Stories from a Curious Traveler
by Laurie McAndish King

ISBN: 978-0-9852672-7-8

First Printing 2014
Printed and bound in the United States of America

For Jim

Contents

INSPIRATION

Preface

Lost? Kidnapped? Eaten alive? Yes, yes, and yes. I was lost without a map in downtown Melbourne (a city of nearly four million people), kidnapped in the scorching Tunisian desert, and eaten alive by swarming mosquitoes in tropical north Queensland, Australia. The 23 tales in this book are all true, and together they tell a larger story: Why I travel.

Well into middle age, I sometimes find myself still trying to *find myself*. Travel is the best way I know do that.

I travel to become lost, confused, disoriented ... and then to find myself again—my most essential self—to realize that I am more than my habits and routines, more than the friends I adore and the foods I prefer, more than my personal history and tenacious assumptions.

I am not a good traveler, though. Even after visiting nearly forty countries, I still worry about what to pack and whether my itinerary needs adjustments. I resent security lines, dislike asking for directions, and abhor anything that makes my motion sickness kick in.

But I travel anyway, because I love being in new places.

Crossing the physical boundaries of states and countries provides an opportunity to stretch my own boundaries. Do I really need a hot shower every morning? What if no one I met today spoke English? How might my perspective about work change if I befriended a Croatian refugee? Because I am experiencing life in a new way, seemingly insignificant events can lead to surprising moments of epiphany.

In Italy, for example, I found beauty at a centuries-old tourist trap, and in Bali my senses of taste and smell were ignited by magical beans. In Costa Rica a bird named Stravinsky got me thinking about destiny, and in Kenya I reconsidered my ideas about cultural differences.

But moments like these are fragile, easily forgotten. And that is why I write: to preserve at least a shadow of those memories and then use them, like meditations, to expand my understanding of the world.

And discovering myself, I want to share my tales.

These are the stories of a woman who grew up in rural America and wanted to see a little more of the world. Along the way I got lost, made mistakes, tried things I would never have done at home, and made a fool of myself. I also experienced great kindnesses and inspiration and insight—not to mention delicious meals—and had a lot of fun.

I hope you'll join me on the journey.

—Laurie McAndish King

The Common Compass, a Laudably Reliable Tool for Wayfinding

LOST
MELBOURNE, AUSTRALIA

They say the Polynesians navigated by squatting low between the two hulls of their ocean-faring canoes, testicles dangling into the water. The combination of ultra-sensitive skin, keen attention to the subtleties of ocean swells, and nautical lore handed down from father to son enabled these ancient tribes to explore the uncharted waters of the South Pacific, and eventually to locate and populate the thousands of tiny islands there.

The Polynesians are not the only culture with impressive navigational abilities. Ancient Phoenicians navigated by the sun and stars, and the Vikings accomplished their feats using mysteriously carved stone disks called *solskuggjáøl*. Aboriginals trekking across the vast Australian Outback navigate using a series of traditional songs and stories called songlines. Each songline designates landmarks such as valleys, rocks, mountains, waterholes, or other contours of the land, allowing the astute Aboriginals, who must have amazing memories, to traverse their great continent without the aid of physical maps. But that is not the most astonishing of their navigational skills, for it is said that Aboriginals living in the Outback can actually smell water from great distances.

My own father has an uncanny ability to align the hour hand of his watch with the shadow of the nearest church steeple and somehow determine which street leads back to his hotel. This seems to work for him anywhere in the northern hemisphere, with the higher latitudes providing the most accurate readings.

For obvious reasons, I have never attempted testicular navigation—and I am not above twisting my lack of that particular navigational aid into an excuse for getting lost. Effective use of celestial bodies, solskuggjáøl, songlines, the scent of water, and church steeple shadows has also eluded me. I still do not own a smart phone, and I find that British-accented smarty-pants who narrates most GPS-based wayfinders impossibly annoying.

The truth is, I have cultivated no navigational abilities or aspirations, because getting lost is such great fun. I love wandering through a new city, with no familiar streets, shops, or restaurants. No nostalgia for—or even local memories of—favorite haunts, old friends and lovers, or lost weekends. I have no profession, no religion, no identity, except what I choose to invent. I can view the world through new eyes, which is one of the great gifts of traveling.

But it means I often spend a great deal of time trying to figure things out—things that ought to be simple enough, like which way is north. In Melbourne, Australia, for example, the Central Business District (CBD) is a grid on an angle; it heads northeast. Even knowing that, I cannot, for the life of me, get my bearings in Melbourne. Partly, it's because the official city map is—for some random reason—rotated ninety degrees clockwise and shows my hotel on the southeast corner of the CBD, when really it's on the northeast. For a while I thought this might be an idiosyncrasy peculiar to the southern hemisphere, perhaps some sort of cartographical counterbalance to the issue of drain water circling in the opposite direction than in the northern hemisphere. But I have discovered that drain water usually—though not always—goes down counterclockwise, no matter which hemisphere you're in. Anyway, it was not just the map that confused me.

One day, after having lived and worked in Melbourne for several months, I began to feel at home, and decided I'd had enough recreational disorientation. I resolved to walk up and down the streets, paying particular attention to the sun at intersections, and, finally, figure out which way was north. The weather was perfect: hot in the sun, cool in the shade, light breeze, bright blue skies. I walked down Exhibition Street, willing myself to achieve some minimal state of orientation, and repeating what I hoped would be a helpful mantra, "South on Exhibition, South on Exhibition, South on Exhibition." But how could I possibly be walking south, with the sun so warm on my back it initiated a little trickle of sweat? Shouldn't it be shining in my eyes? Something felt seriously wrong.

Continuing south on Exhibition Street, I arrived at a corner where the once-grand Southern Cross Hotel was being completely remodeled to include luxury apartments and up-market shopping. Steel I-beams supported scaffolding over the sidewalk, and I considered crossing to the other side, but was more in the mood for a construction site than for the opal stores across the street. The scaffolding would provide cool shade, and I'd seen enough tourist shops for the day.

Someone had spray-painted a message on each consecutive vertical I-beam, drawing the reader in with every step. The first said *Welcome*. Then:

> *Enter*
>
> *Look*
>
> *Read*
>
> *Be Silent*

... each running down an I-beam. Inside the scaffolding, a small gap in the overhanging canvas left room for the artist's message, sprayed in neon orange on plywood:

> *110 million land mines*
>
> *90% war victims are civilians*
>
> *40,000 kids starve to death daily*

1 dead princess

80% W pop = 3rd w ... 80% W goods = 1st w

I may have been lost, but I had found a hidden dimension of Melbourne, a parallel universe in this tidy city with its graffiti discreetly hidden away. How many other worlds existed here, patiently layered, unseen by tourists? How many other ways of seeing, thinking, and understanding played out beneath the city's smooth, genteel surface?

This is why I love to travel: It shakes me out of my routine, provides endless opportunities for experiencing the world anew, and gets right up in my face with tangible evidence that there are many ways to live one's life. In doing so, it forces me to reexamine my perceptual filters, my assumptions and values and direction in life.

I walked on and the I-beams said:

Take it All

Use it All

Shop a Lot

Consume

Forgive

Forget It

No Guilt

Nothing

Suddenly I was out of the scaffolding and back in the bright sunlight. Across the street, a sign announced: *Opals—Australian Souvenirs—Tax Free!!* Around the corner—west on Collins Street—the signs said: *Wedgwood, Waterford, Cartier, Bally, Hermes, Louis Vuitton.*

And there I was, standing in the sunshine, still trying to feel which way was north.

Two Big Cats that Do Not Look Hungry—
But Who Knows for Sure?

Big Cats, No Guns
THE OKAVANGO DELTA, BOTSWANA

The first time I tracked lions, it was from the relative safety and comfort of a large—although open—Land Rover, with a loaded rifle situated handily next to the driver. At that time our guide had assured us that as long as we didn't wear brightly colored clothes, make noise, or stand up, the animals would perceive us as part of the vehicle, and therefore not worth eating. His logic was not entirely convincing. Lions have been making their living—for, what, several million years?—by figuring out what is, or is not, edible. And we were going to fool them by *sitting* instead of standing? I was sure the big cats were smarter than that.

But this safari was different. We were going on foot, and the strict policy at Camp Okavango was *no guns*. Big cats, no guns, traveling on foot ... hmmm.

Adding to my trepidation, our guides, Robert and Rodgers, explained that if we saw lions this morning, they would be hungry, because big cats usually hunt at night. If they were still out stalking prey in the morning, it meant they hadn't found anything to eat the night before. A crazy thought wriggled into my mind: The guides were using us as lion bait. They thought we were clueless American tourists, foolish enough to follow them deep into the big cats' territory with no means of protection. We were. And we did.

Our guides' plan was to travel from our camp by motorboat through the vast delta to another island, and from there to proceed on foot in search of the big cats. Many miles out, through the winding, papyrus-lined waterways, Robert announced excitedly that he had spotted dust in the trees. I didn't see it, even with my binoculars. And I didn't understand what dust had to do with lions. But I went along with the program. We anchored the boat, disembarked, and walked into the remote island's open forest.

This was no Sunday stroll: The tall brown grasses hid hazardous obstacles. Elephants had eaten the relatively tender bark and roots of trees, leaving dead branches and uprooted stumps scattered everywhere. Aardvarks had dug large holes in the ground. Thorns caught on our clothing, and greedy vines grabbed at our legs. And the dung! Everywhere we had to step over dung—all kinds of it, large and small, round and elongated, fresh and dry, in varying stages of decomposition.

I could tell the difference between rhino middens and elephant dung, and was learning to differentiate buffalo from giraffe. Then I saw a new kind of dung: smaller, rounder, fresher—glistening, in fact. Was it lions'? I wondered just how far away the lions actually were, and how close we intended to get. Checking my field guide, I found that lion droppings "are similar to that of the leopard, but larger." This was only marginally more helpful than the entry for elephants, which read, "A good way of testing the freshness of dung, is to thrust your hand into the centre of it. If the dung is fresh, it will be warm inside."

We were a noisy bunch of Americans, and Rodgers ad-monished us to "do *shhh*" and to "talk silently." I noticed that Rodgers and Robert did indeed talk silently, communicating with their eyes and hands that they had heard a noise in this direction, or that they wanted us to walk that way. They reminded me of a TV SWAT team, moving swiftly and efficiently through the bad guy's territory just before the big shootout. Our group, on the other hand, moved like a bunch of Keystone Cops, zig-zagging randomly, tripping in the aardvark holes, backtracking around fallen trees, and fighting back with all our might when vicious vines attacked.

Robert reminded us to walk in single file, always staying together. If we fell back or got out of line, he warned, we'd look smaller and be "on the menu." As if lions haven't had plenty of experience in picking individuals out of a herd. As if they would look hungrily at a line of humans hiking single file and think, "That's just some nasty-tasting giant caterpillar, seriously overburdened with indigestible cameras and binoculars, stumbling slowly and vulnerably through my sovereign territory. Forget it—no chow there."

Most important, Robert said: If a lion did come towards us, "Don't run! Stand your ground!"

Stand my ground?

In the face of a charging lion? What kind of instruction was that? My heart pounded at the thought of it; my legs stiffened, and I wondered whether it would be a good thing to be frozen with fear. My hands began to sweat, and I remembered reading somewhere that humans, dogs, and other mammals whose paws sweat with anxiety do so because the sweat increases friction between the paws and a substrate, allowing for quicker getaways. I was built to run then, *not* to stand my ground!

I stayed near the front of the line, just behind Maureen, a psychiatric nurse from Pittsburgh. Maureen walked with her shoulders slightly hunched, took each step slowly and deliberately, shaded her eyes from the sun as she scanned the distance. I thought she looked like a professional tracker, except for her bright white Asics Gel running shoes—obviously bought new for the trip—and hot pink windbreaker. I had chosen my place carefully: Surely the hot-pink-windbreaker variety of meal would be most tempting. If a lion charged, I would simply maintain my position behind the primary bait.

Maureen's left shoelace was untied. Should I tell her? If I did, she'd stop to tie it, and the whole single-file line would crash into us like a row of dominoes. I would be trampled by my fellow travelers, and perhaps sprain my ankle or fall into a pile of warm dung in the process. If I didn't tell her, Maureen might trip and fall, and be eaten alive.

I kept my mouth shut.

A large, lone bird circled the sky above us. Robert identified it as a white-backed vulture (*Gypus africanus*). Our guides had amazing eyesight. Born and raised in the delta, they could identify all the birds and animals from far away. Soon a second vulture appeared, and then a third. Apparently the vultures knew something we did not.

As we hiked farther into the forest—way too far in to run back to the boat—Robert still saw dust. We kept walking, single file, assiduously staying together, not falling back or getting out of line, doing *shhh*, going deeper and deeper into the forest.

At one point I was tempted to photograph a little bee-eater (*Merops pusillus*), a tiny, brilliantly colored bird with an emerald back and wings, a golden throat, and a brilliant blue "eyebrow." Bee-eaters feast on bees, wasps, and hornets, removing their stingers first by repeatedly hitting the captured insect on a hard surface. These exquisite beauties often make their homes in excavated dirt at the entrance to an aardvark den, and I wanted to stop and hunt for nests. But when I considered the possibility of "death by lion," I decided to stay with the group.

"Listen!" Rodgers and Robert both heard the lions. We kept walking. At first the rest of us didn't hear anything, but a ways farther in we heard a low rumbling sound. "It's the lions! Yes, and they are chasing buffalo!" The rumbling, our guides explained excitedly, was the sound of a thousand hooves. We proceeded, still in line, straining to get a look through the trees at a buffalo or a lion. Suddenly Robert hurried back into our midst, eyes wide and round, and bulging so the whites showed around their whole circumference. "They are coming this way!" he shouted hoarsely. "We are too close! *Go back! Go back!*"

Finally I saw the dust, a huge cloud of it, about 200 yards away and coming towards us fast. It was swirling above a herd of several hundred cape buffalo, and they were coming towards us fast, too. Stampeding, actually.

What was the protocol for a buffalo attack? There was no time to ask. Our careful, single-file line disintegrated into chaos as we ran back—hats, cameras and binoculars flying. No more zigzagging to avoid holes or backtracking around fallen trees; we leapt them all heroically. Several of our group turned out to be talented sprinters, and I personally tested the freshness of five or six piles of dung in the space of twenty seconds.

As suddenly as the stampede began, it was over. It's

interesting, what goes through one's mind at a time like this. As soon as *Escape! Escape!* had run its course, I was overwhelmed with the perfection of Nature's Grand Plan: Elephants knock down large trees, allowing grasslands to develop, which attracts grazing animals, which provide food for the lions. The aardvark holes create natural traps for the lions' prey; the elephants' monumental, nutrient-rich droppings fertilize the tall grasses.... Lost in the beauty of the Grand Plan, it was several minutes before I remembered Maureen. How did her untied shoelace fit in? Had I been homicidally remiss in not mentioning it earlier? Or was I simply playing my predetermined part in the "survival of the fittest"? Did Maureen stand, or did she run? Had she been trampled by stampeding buffalo, eaten by a hungry lion?

I came to my senses, surveyed the scene, and saw Maureen's hot pink jacket halfway up a small tree, with Maureen still inside it. Apparently it had not provoked the lions. We began to regroup, and everyone seemed to have survived. The cape buffalo—still about seventy yards away—had also survived. They had all stopped running and were now milling about restlessly. They seemed to be more afraid of us than of the charging lions. This did not strike me as an effective adaptive behavior, but what do I know about the life of a buffalo? And what did they know about humans? At any rate, they kept their eyes on us and on the lions, which—conveniently—made it easy for us to keep track of the five adult lions that were now in our immediate vicinity.

Make that five *hungry* adult lions.

I had heard that female lions form hunting bands, and that the males don't bother to assist them. But this was a group of four females and one large male with an impressive golden mane. What was *he* doing there? He was probably so famished that he couldn't even wait for the females to make a kill. He was big, that was for sure. I couldn't see his teeth, but I know they were long and sharp, and I'll bet he was salivating.

I smelled the dust. Dust, and a sweat-like smell. Was it the buffalo, or the lions? Was it me? Was it fear? The lions were not yet attacking, so I had a moment to contemplate: *Should I turn and run, or stand and scream? Would it make a difference? Do I have a choice?*

I would like to report that Rodgers and Robert were unfazed, but that would not be entirely true. Actually, they looked anxious. They had no guns. They were responsible for a dozen travelers. And we were seventy yards away from five hungry lions.

The big cats paced around the edges of the buffalo herd, eyeing one individual, then another. What if one looked at me? Should I make eye contact, or avoid it? I began to feel panicky. Robert's words echoed in my mind: *If a lion does come towards you, don't run!* Legs locked, I stood my ground, and felt proud of myself for having the presence of mind to follow instructions in a crisis. But then it occurred to me: *If I stood my ground, and everyone else retreated, did that make me clever? Or did it make me lion food?*

Fortunately, my survival did not depend on my own intelligence: Rodgers and Robert took control, instructing us to remain facing the lions and walk slowly backwards, away from them. We did so. Soon, it was OK to turn and walk—a bit more quickly—back to the boat. When we were safely on board, and motoring back to camp, I marveled at the beauty of Nature's Grand Plan, at green papyrus against intense azure skies and the deliciousness of a bottle of cold Chibuku Shake-Shake beer.

Life is good, when you're not on the menu.

Stravinsky, the Fiery-billed Aracari, from His Good Side

STRAVINSKY'S GIFT

LA GUÁCIMA, COSTA RICA

Stravinsky stretches languidly, neck to toe, then falls onto his butt. With only one useful leg and no tail feathers to speak of, his balance is compromised. He cannot perch. He is forced to live on the floor of his cage, hopping on one foot, tail feathers worn to nubs. The flight feathers on each glossy green wing—which should be long and elegant—are also shortened from constant rubbing against the floor. They give this small toucan the sad, stunted look of a multiple amputee.

Peering into Stravinsky's cage, I am immediately drawn to him, although I cannot say why. Perhaps I identify with his melancholy. Or maybe I know, somehow, that he has a gift for me. But Stravinsky will not make eye contact—his only acknowledgement of my presence is a nervous hop to the far side of his cage. I wish the skittish creature would reciprocate my interest.

We have come together at Finca Fango de la Suerte, the sprawling central Costa Rican home of Joan Hall and Lenny Karpman, who have created a sanctuary here for more than forty injured and unwanted animals. The climate is nearly perfect, the air is clear, and the *finca* exudes a warm, amiable hospitality. Stravinsky has lived here for three years, recuperating from his wounds. I am visiting for two weeks, craving sanctuary myself.

I love the name of the place: A *finca* is a small ranch, and *fango de la suerte* translates roughly as *lucky mud*. It's a reference to *Cat's Cradle*, the Kurt Vonnegut, Jr. novel in which God created the earth and then woke up the mud so it could see what an excellent job he had done. "And I was some of the mud that got to sit up and look around. Lucky me, lucky mud ... I loved everything I saw!"

Joan and Lenny love everything they see, too. They have brought homeless cats, dogs, and birds to Finca Fango de la Suerte. The place is a tropical madhouse. Roosters crow at midnight and kittens eat butter off the breakfast table. Parrots laugh raucously and screech "Grandpa! Grandpa!" when Lenny walks by. Six dogs lick my feet and legs at every opportunity. Their tongues are long and soft.

But it is Stravinsky, a fiery-billed aracari, who captivates me. A riff of red across the small toucan's golden breast conjures blood, as though he'd recently lost a fight. Stravinsky *won* a fight, though—a fierce

The fiery-billed aracari (*Pteroglossus frantzii*) breeds only on the Pacific slopes of southern Costa Rica and western Panama.

one. Years ago, he was attacked as a nestling by a marauding rat, which gnawed all the toes off the

20

tiny bird's right foot after brutally devouring his sibling and nest mate in its entirety. Left alone, Stravinsky would have starved to death—if he had not been eaten first by a snake, a coati, or another rat. But Stravinsky was saved, and brought to Amigos de las Aves, a rambling avian rescue center founded by Richard and Margot Frisius on the slopes of the Costa Rican rainforest. In the wild, small flocks of fiery-billed aracaris forage for fruit and insects in the humid forests. As many as five adults sleep together in old woodpecker holes—tails folded over their backs—and share parenting responsibilities. At Amigos de las Aves, the parenting responsibilities fall to Richard and Margot. Their witty name for the bird—Stravinsky—was a nod to the great composer's *Firebird*.

Maybe it was more than a nod. Stravinsky-the-composer was evolution in action: restless, curious, experimental, moving listeners through chaos to complexity. His intention for *The Rite of Spring*, for example, was to produce a "bloodcurdling" masterpiece evoking the unsentimental savagery of the natural world. *Firebird* is uncharacteristically melodic, a respite from Stravinsky's dissonant style, just as Amigos de las Aves is a respite from the realities its inhabitants face in the wild.

Underfunded, Amigos de las Aves could not provide the high level of ongoing care Stravinsky required. So he moved to Lenny and Joan's *finca*. Lenny built a special cage with a high floor and an orthopedic perch. He situated it near the kitchen door, so the forlorn bird would have regular company and eye-level stimulation. Stravinsky eschewed his special perch, but gradually developed a relationship with Joan and Lenny.

Lenny introduces me to Stravinsky one morning at dawn, and I watch as the bird hops on his one good foot and balances on the stump that is his other leg. He doesn't screech like the larger birds, but chatters a quiet greeting. Lenny feeds Stravinsky a few slices of banana and fills his bowl with diced watermelon, pineapple and papaya. Stravinksy eats the banana first. It's his favorite food.

The next day, Joan opens the cage door and shows me how she makes a game with the first two fingers of her left hand, scissoring Stravinsky's beak. He stutters softly and nudges back, caressing her fingers with his beak. Then Stravinsky licks her fingers with his slim brown tongue. Joan says he likes the salt from her skin. She tosses a single piece of kitty kibble toward Stravinsky and he catches it in mid-air. They play well together.

That evening when all the other birds perch, both feet locked in sleep, Stravinsky slides his long, elegant bill through the bars of his cage and leans against it for support. That beak is a beauty: The upper mandible is vermillion, fading like a sunset to yellow-green, and then again to violet at the base. A crisp daffodil-colored band marks the line where bill meets face on Stravinsky's left side—his good side—but runs ragged and muddy on the right.

I wanted to learn more about Stravinsky, so Joan and Lenny took me to visit Amigos de las Aves, the eight-acre rescue center where the bird grew up. It began as the Flor de Mayo botanical preserve, founded by Sir Charles Lancaster, renowned naturalist and botanist to Queen Victoria. Sending exotic specimens home from the colonies was a noble scientific pursuit, and Lancaster procured thousands of plants from Central America for the Royal Botanic Gardens at Kew, which now boasts the world's largest collection of living plants.

Today Flor de Mayo's history is commemorated by a single, modest wrought-iron sign that uses a few weak curlicues to decorate the rusting letters of the words *Flor de Mayo*. The dark, damp grounds are populated with tall palms, giant climbing philodendrons, and uncountable epiphytes—plants that depend on others for their physical support. Orchids hide their beauty in the dripping undergrowth.

Richard and Margot transformed the silent botanical preserve into a lively avian rescue center, Amigos de las Aves. The couple had relocated to Costa Rica in 1980 with their own menagerie of exotic birds, some of which they acquired when Richard worked in

Africa for Pan Am. Richard built special outdoor cages for the birds, using wire screening with squares of just the right size for the birds' feet to grasp comfortably.

The couple's reputation as animal rescuers and rehabilitators grew, and now Amigos de las Aves is inhabited by hundreds of "donated" birds—former pets who turned out to be too noisy, too smelly or too aggressive for their owners' tastes. Parrots, macaws and other colorful exotic birds who were confiscated from poachers—presumably destined for the illegal pet trade—ended up here, too. Many of the birds at Amigos de las Aves can be re-released, if habitat is available. Some, like Stravinsky, cannot.

The great green macaw is also called Buffon's macaw.

Amigos de las Aves specializes in the rescue and breeding of macaws. I saw at least two hundred there. One of the species they shelter, the great green macaw, is the second-largest parrot in the world; its wingspan is well over a meter. In the wild, great greens can live for more than fifty years. They usually fly in pairs or in small groups; these birds have family values.

Millions of great green macaws once migrated between Honduras and Ecuador, their flight following the fruiting of the *almendro*, or wild almond tree. Today, ornithologists estimate there are at most 250 individuals left in the wild, and fewer than a third of those are breeding pairs. Amigos de las Aves is the only place that has been able to breed great greens in captivity. But successful captive breeding does not solve the problem. There is nowhere for the great green macaws to go.

Logging has destroyed most of their habitat. Seventy of Amigos de las Aves's great greens are ready for release now, awaiting appropriate sites. They need an adequate natural food supply, nesting sites, and the guaranteed safety of a private lodge or protected reserve. In the meantime, most live in small cages, too crowded to mate. Overcrowding makes them cranky. The longer the macaws are here, the more difficult it will be for them to find food in the wild, to build nests, reproduce and avoid predation. The staff and volunteers at Amigos de las Aves are searching for release sites.

The visit left me discouraged, but Joan was philosophical. "The macaws are not destined to live on this earth for very long," she said.

The next morning, Lenny feeds Stravinsky his fruit. Stravinksy begins eating the banana, but when Lenny moves on too quickly to feed the other birds, Stravinsky stops eating and bangs the bars of his cage with his beak in protest. Lenny returns and rubs Stravinsky's outstretched bill with one finger, petting the top of his tiny head with another. They have developed a sweet ritual.

The days pass, and I continue to visit Stravinksy. I learn to stand a few feet back from the cage, so as not to frighten him. I speak quietly, tell him where I live, muse about the weather and upcoming elections. I admire the rhythmic pattern of shallow, saw-like serrations along the edge of his powerful bill; they would have been useful for feeding in the wild. In the evenings I stop by to bid Stravinsky goodnight, but he is usually already asleep.

One warm afternoon Stravinsky bathes in front of me, balanced on one foot, his short dark wings beating like miniature outboard motors, wet belly feathers wilting in a bedraggled mess. He uses his beak to splash water out of the shallow bowl in his cage. The spray is cool, and I feel as though we were bathing together, Stravinsky and I.

Afterwards, I watch Stravinsky hobble over to his fruit bowl. He stumbles once, then continues. The little bird picks up a cube of watermelon with the very tip of his bill. In one fluid motion, he opens his beak, tosses the fleshy fruit back into his mouth, and swallows. Then he picks up a second watermelon chunk, hops back over to where I stand watching and extends his bill out through the black cage bars toward me. He is still holding the watermelon.

Is Stravinsky offering me his food—food that he cannot catch for himself, that he is dependent on Joan and Lenny to provide? If so, I am humbled by such trust and generosity. I am also perplexed: Lenny had asked me not to feed the birds, but he hadn't said what to do if a bird tried to feed me. Should I accept the soft, pink piece of fruit? I am not as trusting as Stravinsky is. I back away from the gentle aracari and his powerful, serrated beak.

Stravinsky looks at me and waits, a large drop of liquid wobbling at the base of his bill. It looks like a teardrop. He balances on one leg with his good side facing me. I look back and reconsider. The red band across Stravinsky's belly reminds me of the belt on a swashbuckling pirate. His eyes shine clear and curious, with an inky pupil polka-dotting the center of each bright white eye. That droplet on Stravinsky's beak is not a tear; it is juice from the watermelon. I step closer and smile at the plucky bird. He had a rough start, but life is good here in the land of lucky mud.

Lenny approaches the cage, sticks his finger in, and strokes the bird's back. Contented, Stravinsky closes his eyes, tilts his head, and purrs.

A Greater Bamboo Lemur, Just Beginning to Decimate a Patch of Bamboo Behind the Outhouse

Lemurs and Leeches
RANOMAFANA, MADAGASCAR

I was in the outhouse, with my pants halfway down, when I heard an urgent whisper outside: "Bamboo lemur, behind the loo!" I made a judgment call. The greater bamboo lemur (*Hapalemur simus*) is one of the rarest primates in the world; researchers believe there are fewer than 1,000 individuals left. In fact, this critically endangered species was believed to be extinct until it was rediscovered only a few years ago. Never mind the loo—I rushed out, hoping for a quick look.

The lemurs had teddybear-like faces, round chestnut-colored eyes, and fluffy, pale grey ear tufts that made them look like little Yodas. Several came right down to eye level and sat only an arm's length away, watching us nonchalantly as they broke giant bamboo stalks, stripping off the tough outer layers and munching the inner pith. Greater bamboo lemurs have adapted to process cyanide-laced bamboo, and thus occupy a rare and peculiar ecological niche.

This was nothing like seeing animals in captivity—through glass or bars, or across a wide moat—wondering about their adaptation to zoo trees and zoo food and zoo neighbors.

This was the real thing! I could have reached out and touched their soft gray fur, or rubbed them behind the ears like my cat. I might have tried, too, except that teeth made for eating bamboo clearly mean business, and these were wild animals. My heart pounded with excitement, and I watched for more than an hour as five lemurs moved methodically from one stout stalk to the next, wreaking havoc on the bamboo grove. This species requires a large territory.

I was in Madagascar, with a group of Earthwatchers who had volunteered to help Dr. Patricia Wright collect field data for a study of *Propithecus diadema edwardsi* at Ranomafana National Park. Perhaps you know *Propithecus* by its common name, the Milne-Edwards' sifaka. Well, perhaps not. But surely you're familiar with lemurs, those cute, monkey-like prosimians found only in Madagascar. Like almost all plants and animals there, lemurs are in danger of extinction; conservation efforts during the next few years will be critical for their survival.

Dr. Wright—whose interest in primate research was whetted by a pair of pet Peruvian monkeys she owned as a young housewife in Brooklyn—has been studying lemurs since 1984. Her vision and hard work were largely responsible for the establishment of Ranomafana National Park, and she was awarded both the MacArthur "genius" grant and Madagascar's *Chevalier d'Ordre National* (the equivalent of knighthood) for her efforts there. I felt honored to be working with Dr. Wright.

Honored and smelly. Gary, Pam, Christine and I ("Team 3") ran through the rainforest together, sweating profusely, for two weeks. Our legs grew strong, as did our odor. We had to move fast to keep up with the lemurs; every day they led us through the forest, off the trail, down steep, vine-covered slopes, across a tributary of the Namorona River, along the rocky bank, back across the river—several times—through the tangled undergrowth, and back up the river's slippery slopes. I couldn't help but think they were toying with us.

Not only that, but the rainforest was teeming with stinging caterpillars, malaria-carrying mosquitoes, biting horseflies, and blood-sucking leeches. Spiders the size of my fist were common, and I was regularly attacked at dinner by moths bigger than a hummingbird.

When we first arrived at the jungle outpost, I noticed that some of our guides smelled pretty ripe. I figured on keeping my distance until I got used to it. Little did I know that I—and all my fellow Earthwatchers who had arrived fresh, clean, and eager—would soon smell of sweat and mildew and boiled zebu meat.

Twelve of us, strangers from around the world, had volunteered two weeks of our precious vacation time to track lemurs in the service of environmental science.

Our group included a pharmacist, a private pilot, a dentist, two bored housewives, a member of the British Royal Air Force, several avid birders, and me—a nature-lover since childhood—plus a handful of graduate students working on research projects. I fantasized that the pharmacist's large backpack transformed, with the push of a button, into a James Bond-issue collapsible stretcher, which would be useful if I slipped on the wet trails, tumbled down the mountain, caught my foot in a treacherous vine, and broke my leg. The pilot could evacuate me on the collapsible stretcher in an emergency, although we would need to find an airplane first.

Even though we were a varied bunch, our reasons for participating were the same: We all cared deeply about the environment, and saw this as a way to express our commitment with action. Several of us (including myself) were at mid-life transitions, and wanted—needed—to do something that would have a real impact on the world. And we were each hungry for adventure. Why *this* adventure? Because Madagascar can't wait. Whole ecosystems are dying, and species are becoming extinct. We were there to save the world.

Our headquarters for this grand endeavor was a one-room log cabin. It was packed with an assortment of blue plastic tarps and leaky tents, paperback travel stories in several languages, hiking boots that fit everyone and no one, precarious stacks of field data books, and damp, patient messages awaiting researchers who were somewhere deep in the forest. There was also a closet-like pantry, stocked with delicious-smelling local honey, tins of sweetened condensed milk, and a few recycled jars filled with sugary peanut butter, generously donated by the wife of one of our Malagasy guides. We slept in the leaky tents.

Although we had been warned to expect pit toilets, we found two semi-private outhouses, with toilets that flushed most of the time. The only other permanent structures in camp were four shower stalls, in which hundreds of tiny gray spiders had taken up residence. We used these facilities with a sort of grateful trepidation.

After the lemur-by-the-outhouse incident, I discovered a small black leech attached to my right hip. I must have got it in the outhouse, somehow, and not noticed because of my rush to see the greater bamboo lemur. Anyway, I brushed it off—with minimal bloodshed—and quickly warned the rest of the group, "I got a leech, and it was in my underwear!"

"I hope you divorced him!" the dentist shot back, and the researchers, who lived in the jungle for months at a time, proceeded to tell their leech encounter stories: Debi woke up in the middle of the night, unable to breathe, with a blood-swollen leech up her nose; Becky once had to pull one off her tongue, and

Sarah got one of those stealthy little critters on her eyeball (it had been on the eyepiece of her binoculars). These rainforest leeches are small and terrestrial, which means you're never safe from them, even at night, all zipped up inside your sleeping bag and tent. But I found that with leeches—like many things—the anticipation is far worse than the actual experience.

Madagascar today is a conservation hotspot; most of the rainforest is gone, and many of the unique species here are in imminent danger of extinction. Although international money is flowing into the country, not enough finds its way to the local people, and centuries-old patterns of *tavy* (slash-and-burn farming) are almost impossible to change. In a subsistence-level economy with inadequate health care and education, it's difficult to convince people to switch to sustainable agriculture. The little rainforest that remains is under tremendous pressure, since the rapidly growing Malagasy population needs land to produce food.

The lemurs we followed are almost totally arboreal, eating, sleeping, and traveling in the treetops. If trees are removed—either by selective logging or by clear cutting—resulting gaps in the forest canopy restrict the lemurs' territory, and their movement within their territory. This is true even if primary forest has been replaced by secondary growth; it's old-growth trees—ones that have been around for hundreds of years—that are intertwined with the vines and lianas so important for arboreal locomotion. Forest degradation is also a problem because these tree-dwelling animals don't have adaptive strategies for dealing with predators on the ground.

My job was to collect data. Every ten minutes, I used my Rite-in-the-Rain pen to record an adult female lemur's behavior in a waterproof field data book. What was she doing: feeding, grooming, resting, or traveling? What kind of tree was she in, and how high? If she was feeding, was it on fruit, seeds, flowers, or leaves? I also recorded the focal lemur's nearest (lemur) neighbor, and distance to nearest neighbor, which will eventually help researchers understand more about the relationship between diet and social structure.

Our Malagasy guides were essential; they were experts at tracking lemurs as they leapt from vine to vine and scampered up and down trees. They knew the names of all the plants, and were good at estimating height. (Whereas I found myself wondering how many men stacked on top of one another would equal the height of the lemurs' treetop feeding spot—five tall men? six?—and then doubling the number to convert to meters.)

My guide was Dominique, a short, brown man with shy eyes who moved quickly and easily through the rainforest. He seemed completely at home there, and very different from the volunteers—large, white people who crashed through the undergrowth and tripped over vines. Following along right after Dominique, I imagined that I picked up some of his gracefulness and agility; it was so easy to walk with him through the forest!

Later, I realized it was easy because Dominique discretely pushed lianas out of my way, pointed out thorns and perilous holes in the forest floor, and subtly sliced the occasional threatening vine with a pocketknife hidden in his hand. We didn't speak the same language, but Dominique's actions communicated his generous nature. When we crossed the river, he balanced carefully on dry stones so I'd know where to step, even though he was wearing waterproof rubber boots. (I was not.)

Why bring foreigners into the country to track lemurs? Although the local Malagasy people know the rainforest very well, they have a decidedly non-Western approach to data collection. Our conceptions of time, accuracy, consistency, and detail are not theirs. And Dr. Wright needs to collect a lot of data. The more researchers understand about lemurs' lives, the more successful they are likely to be in figuring out how humans and lemurs can live together. And by focusing attention on lemurs and other endangered species, we encourage the Malagasy people to preserve the remaining rainforest.

Most of the island's wide range of plants and animals—more than 200,000 species—have evolved in isolation from the rest of the world. If you don't count birds, which can fly there from mainland Africa, more than eighty percent of Madagascar's plants and animals are endemic—found nowhere else on earth.

Madagascar's evolutionary history is complicated and paradoxical. How can it be that this island, only 270 miles off the eastern coast of Africa, shares none of the continent's large mammals, such as elephants, antelopes, or lions? Or that it has only one insectivore, the tenrec, a hedgehog-like creature whose nearest relative is native to Cuba and Haiti?

Collecting field data for Dr. Wright was not easy. I was always hot and tired, sweating and thirsty, and desperate for a shower. My glasses fogged up during the daytime, and every item of clothing I took ended up smelling—either vaguely or distinctly—of mildew. I paid good money to spend two weeks of my life chasing lemurs and recording their most mundane behaviors.

The female tailless common tenrec, by the way, can produce up to 32 offspring at a time—the record for mammals—and individuals have been recorded with up to 29 nipples. Tenrecs' super fecundity is more than an interesting curiosity, though. It helps explain the wild speciation they have undergone on the island. Lemurs, chameleons, finch-like vangas, and palm trees have also produced far more variety than taxonomists would expect in such a small area.

But I love the rainforest. I love the souimanga sunbird's high warble, the insistent "come sunshine, welcome sunshine" of the cuckoo, the rushing Namorona River, the greenness of the canopy over-head, and the tangle of vines underfoot. I am fascinated by the unique wild-life and unearthly landscapes in Madagascar. And I have discovered that even blood-sucking leeches aren't so bad, after the initial, getting-to-know-you phase of the relationship.

I volunteered because the lemurs are endangered, and collecting ecological data is an important first step in helping to preserve their habitat. I'll return because I want to see the people who live in Madagascar remain in their forest home, despite growing economic and ecological pressures. And because rainforests are the earth's lungs, and my grandchildren will need to breathe.

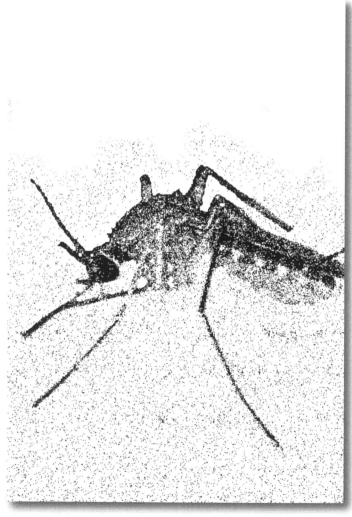

A Blood-Sucking Beast, Which I'm Sure God Created for a Reason, Although I cannot Imagine What it Would Be

The Truth about Eco-Travel
THE DAINTREE, QUEENSLAND

Jim was hesitant right from the start.

"Cape Tribulation? *Wilderness Area?* No way!"

Our travel agent had provided a bright, glossy brochure of the Bunyip Lodge, and I cajoled my husband into going along to this eco-resort in northern Australia. "Eco-tourism" sounded so romantic: waking to the trill of morning birdsong, viewing exotic animals without binoculars, and falling asleep to the melodic sounds of the night forest. Who could resist two weeks in a pristine rainforest? I reminded my metro man that there was a *resort* in eco-resort, and assured him that any inconveniences would be minor. Besides, the brochure featured a photo of a sparkling swimming pool. If Jim decided against traipsing through the rainforest with me, he could always relax by the pool.

I wanted to be one with the rainforest.

We traveled twelve thousand miles by air and bus, transferred to a precarious wooden ferry to cross the Daintree River's gaping mouth, and finished our journey in an eight-passenger minibus that rattled and shivered and shimmied along a deeply rutted road. So far, so good. But, arriving at the Bunyip Lodge in late evening, we began to discover the truth about eco-tourism. The minibus would not fit on the "resort's" overgrown road, so the driver was forced to deposit us—rather unceremoniously, I thought—at the side of a road that cut a thin ribbon through dense jungle. There were no lights at the unmarked drop-off point and, as the minibus quivered off to its next destination, we found ourselves standing alone—in complete darkness—with our luggage.

We hadn't packed flashlights. Who would think we'd need one to get to the hotel lobby? Jim and I stood stupidly in place for a few minutes as our eyes adjusted, and eventually discovered a path leading through the jungle to a faint light. Leaving our luggage heaped in a pile, we stumbled down the bumpy, vine-tangled trail towards the resort. *The porters can retrieve it later,* I thought.

Although there was no lobby, we did manage to track down the proprietor, an amiable fellow called Tony, who was unable to check us in because the computer was down.

"A bug?" I sympathized, remembering the last time my own computer had crashed.

"Nawr—it's the bloody mice. They've chewed right through the wires again," Tony explained. Ever helpful, he lent us a couple of torches so we could retrieve our luggage and carry it to the cabin.

There were no porters.

Jim and I were both dripping with sweat before we had walked the 100 yards from drop-off point to office. But we remained optimistic, and decided that although the weather and accommodations were not exactly what we had anticipated, it would be fine as long as there was air conditioning.

Of course, there was none.

There *were* cracks in the walls wide enough for a small dog to pass through—surely these were not for wildlife viewing—and a narrow bed surrounded by alarming volumes of mosquito netting (never a good sign). There was also a plasticized placard in the room requesting that we leave the lights and ceiling fan on at all times to inhibit the encroachment of creeping jungle rot. Occupying a prominent position on the tiny bathroom counter was a super-sized red box of salt, along with instructions for using it to remove leeches: "Simply rub the salt over the attached leech...."

Jim and I sank onto the bed and turned to face each other. He beat me to the question: "Whose idea *was* this, anyway?"

It was time for some serious attitude adjustment. We ambled over to the open-air bar, sucked down a couple of gin and tonics, and flipped through the limp pages of several field guides we found stacked on the barstools—a makeshift library. (Suddenly, I understood why the local currency had a high plastic content: plain paper does not hold up in such high humidity.) Bats swooped precipitously overhead. This was my kind of place after all: Even the bar celebrated flora and fauna.

I planned to search for the rare buff-breasted paradise kingfisher. "It migrates all the way from New Guinea," the guidebook said, "to breed only in this small area in North Queensland, and nests by burrowing into termite mounds." I would also be on the lookout for the musky rat kangaroo, a "rat-sized" marsupial that looks like a miniature kangaroo, climbs trees, hops like a rabbit, and commonly nests in the dreaded wait-a-while plant (more on that to come). The third animal I hoped to spot was the cassowary, an ostrichlike bird that can kick a person to death in self-defense. It wasn't entirely clear, from the text, whether death resulted from the power of the kick itself, or from the sharp nails on the bird's inner toes, which "can easily rip human flesh." Now *this* was exciting.

The cassowary, I learned, is Australia's largest land animal, weighing as much as 130 pounds. Not surprisingly, it is quite incapable of flight. Vestigial wings each carry three to five wire-like feathers, which are used to help brush aside undergrowth as the cassowary travels through the rainforest. As it moves, the giant bird lowers its head "for protection" and "lifts its toes right up under its chin." I couldn't fathom what a gigantic, man-killing bird might need protection from—except, perhaps, humans, as it is an endangered species, with fewer than 1,500 individuals remaining. The male cassowary incubates eggs and cares for the young, which I hope bodes well for the survival of the species.

But larger-than-human size, a comical gait, and killer toenails are just the beginning of the cassowary's odd characteristics. It also sports body feathers that look like foot-and-a-half-long strands of luxurious taupe-colored fur, a bright blue neck, a long red wattle, and a head crowned with a large casque or "helmet" of horn-covered cartilage, the size of which is believed to be significant in determining the cassowary's social status. And let's not forget the bird's "uniquely short digestive system," which allows it to eat the fruits of poisonous plants and eliminate the toxins before absorbing them. In fact, seeds often remain intact, and can grow after passing through the cassowary, which plays an essential part in the dispersion of seeds from up to one hundred species of trees and shrubs. Other rainforest inhabitants—notably the musky rat kangaroo—commonly include partially-digested fruit from the cassowary's droppings in their diets. This bird—shy, fast-moving, and integral to the ecosystem—had captured my imagination. Here was a creature worth viewing, and I was eager to begin the search.

Not wanting to be outdone, Jim studied up on the local flora. "It says there's something called the gimpy-gimpy plant that causes horses to commit suicide."

"Does not," I countered. Surely he was kidding.

"*Duh-zz.* Page 137. The most terrifying plant in the area," Jim read, "is the gimpy-gimpy. When brushed against, its leaves release an extremely painful irritant. There is no known antidote, and the pain can last for months."

"All right, but what about the horses?" I interrupted, catching him in what was surely a complete fabrication.

"Horses have been known to die from charging into trees after exposure to this plant," he continued. "The leaves appear soft and fuzzy from a distance, and have been used, by some stunningly unfortunate explorers, as rainforest toilet paper."

Ouch.

Second on the dangerous-to-horses-and-other-large-mammals list is the "wait-a-while" tree, also called "lawyer cane" because, once hooked by the thorns on this pitiless plant, one is as irretrievably entangled as if involved in the legal process. The vegetation starts out looking like a small palm tree, then grows long, wiry "tendrils" which are decidedly not tender—they're lined with rows of viciously sharp barbed hooks. If you happen to brush past one of these possessive forest dwellers, it grabs your clothing and holds on tightly until you back up and remove the thorns. The tree has even been known to "pull people off horses and motorcycles" as they ride by. Eventually, the long, barbed vine-like part grows to an inch or more in diameter, the thorns drop off, and the result is the smoothly-benign rattan from which patio chairs were made in the 1970s.

Over another round of gin and tonics, Jim and I anticipated the next day's activities, which now revolved around avoiding terrifying plant life. "We might be lucky enough to spot a dusky-colored, rat-like kangaroo scampering about in the rainforest shadows," I enthused. "It's the world's most primitive marsupial!"

"Yes, and we could also see a small brown bird covered with termites, or a large brown bird that could kick us to death," Jim replied, with somewhat less exuberance. "*These* were the exotic native species you had dreamed of encountering?"

Next morning, the air remained thick. The shirts we had worn the day before and hung in front of the window to air out remained wet—not merely damp, but soaked through—with perspiration.

Everything inside our suitcases was wet, too, so Jim used a hairdryer on our shorts and shirts. Then we headed for the lodge, where I scouted around for the inviting swimming pool that had been featured in the brochure. Desperate to float in it, I imagined diving in, a brisk splash, then full-body relief.

The pool did not exist.

Oh, there was a tiny wading hole, similar in overall look, if not dimension, to the palatial pool featured in the brochure. The photographer had apparently taken the shot from ground level, and used an extremely wide-angle lens, in order to flatter the tiny pond and lure unsuspecting tourists.

Tony was sympathetic and let us in on a secret, suggesting that we spend the morning "cooling your inner core," as the locals did, by soaking in Cooper's Creek just down the hill. He assured us that the leeches there were only small, the kind that bite you gently and then fall off. "Just a little nibble, really. No worries."

The photo-perfect swimming hole was clear and beautiful, surrounded by lush tropical vegetation, shaded by magnificent rainforest trees. And the water was cold, as Tony had promised.

Very, *very* cold.

I'm a bit of a baby about plunging my body into frigid leech-filled streams, so it took me a good twenty minutes to submerge. My feet were easy, lower legs not so bad. Thighs difficult, waist nearly impossible. The water was unbearably cold, and I kept thinking about the leeches, and which of my body parts they would be most likely to attach themselves to. Did they prefer light or dark? Cold or warmth? Freedom to crawl around or the protection of a cozy nook or cranny?

With my mind finally off the oppressive heat I relaxed, looked around, and began to think: *Who would live in a place like this, anyway? Were they all insane? Had they been kicked out of other towns, or even other countries?* Visions of early shiploads of convicts filled my mind. Perhaps the crazy ones had migrated to the hinterlands of Queensland? But no—everyone we had met seemed quite civilized.

An intense vibration interrupted my reverie, and I realized my teeth were chattering uncontrollably. After sitting in the numbingly-cold creek for more than an hour, we had unwittingly induced hypothermia. *This* was the locals' strategy for surviving in a sweltering climate!

But I did finally feel better—especially after removing the small leech that clung tenderly to my right big toe. So much better, in fact, that we decided to take a nature walk. Tony drove us to a nearby nature reserve and introduced us to Helen, a stout, hobbit-like woman with the air of someone who had spent a few too many years alone in the jungle. Although the sun was shining and the blue sky showed no hint of rain, she dressed in a bright yellow slicker and knee-high gumboots for our rainforest walk.

We traipsed for hours through lush rainforest suffused with dim green luminescence. In some places the sun barely filtered through, and light seemed to emanate from mossy surfaces and dew-covered leaves. Primeval cycads—a primitive plant whose existence dates back 250 million years—stood in groves, water dripping from their palm-like fronds. Ulysses butterflies, brilliant blue, with four-inch wingspans, floated silently by. I was in heaven.

Jim did not share my appreciation of the living museum surrounding us, home to some of the world's rarest plants and animals. "I think we've seen all 3,000 endemic species," he muttered from behind me on the trail. "Now I only need to sit on a gimpy-gimpy plant to make my trip complete."

Then we came upon what were clearly Helen's favorites: ants swarming by the thousands along rough tree branches. Each ant was about a quarter of an inch long, and had a delicate, bright green abdomen that was grossly over-extended—filled with nectar the ant had collected—and looked as though it was about to burst. Helen gently pulled an extra-large-sized ant off a tree and extended it, posterior end first, to within inches of my face. "'Ere ya go, then. Go ahead, lick its butt."

Lick the ant's butt?

I don't know whether I was more afraid of the ant, with its horrifyingly engorged abdomen, or of Helen and her curiously insistent attitude. She touched the ant's translucent bulge to her own confidently out-stretched tongue, and I bravely followed suit. After it was clear I had not been poisoned, Jim licked his own ant, and his eyes shot open. The taste was like mixing the intense fizz of an Alka Seltzer with tangy lime sherbet.

Helen explained that the ants were great to have around, because they kept other bugs away. I was glad to hear this, as I'm always the first to know when mosquitoes are nearby: they apparently sense the sweetness of my blood, or the depth of my hatred for their species, and swarm about me without fail.

Despite the ants, today was no exception. The mosquitoes swarmed, they landed, and they sucked my blood mercilessly. We convinced Helen to turn back just as it began to rain. Venomous tree frogs croaked a deafening chorus that echoed in every direction and disoriented me completely. Water gushed down in torrents, and my respect for Helen's sartorial eccentricities increased. Our feet sank into calf-deep mud, which threatened my balance and oozed its way down to the very toes of my new Blundstone hiking boots. My bare arms and legs itched wildly.

That's when I realized my wish had been granted. Although we had not spotted the elusive cassowary, I had licked an ant's butt, and I had provided nourishing blood for the local mosquitoes and leeches. I had melted in the heat and been numbed by the creek, been thrown off balance in eons-old mud and disoriented by echoing frogsong.

I had become one with the rainforest.

The next morning I counted more than seventy-five bites on the lower half of my left leg alone. I spent the following week suffering grievously, and experimenting with every imaginable remedy for itching, none of which was particularly effective, although topical gin was a contender. But *this* is the trip we will remember forever. When I reminded him of it several years later, Jim replied, "Let's go back!"

Lovers at Saint-Germaine l'Auxerrois in Paris, Who I had to Watch for Several Minutes in Order to Get this Photo, Even though they were Not Moving Very Much

French Kiss

PARIS, FRANCE

You will only require three things for your trip to Paris: spray-on jeans, a large bag—even if you are a small person—and ballet flats. This authoritative advice was posted on an I-♥-Paris-type website aimed at helping travelers enjoy their Parisian visits. I began to worry almost immediately.

Even though I'd look fine in tight jeans, I won't be caught dead in them for a multitude of reasons. Comfort, my sense of modesty, and yeast infections spring to mind. I could easily lose a small pet in my own medium-sized bag, so a large one is definitely out. And ballet flats in a city of walkers? Well, that strikes me as just plain dumb.

On the other hand, I didn't want to look like a gauche American tourist in this city of Chanel, Guerlain and Dior. Were there any other options for fitting in? Do tight pants, enormous handbags and shoes without arch support really define the Parisian woman? Just what is the *quoi* in her *je ne sais quoi*? Is it all about the way she looks, or is there something more subtle? I wanted to find out.

My research began with Françoise, my Parisian host and a good friend of a good friend. I was couch-surfing at Françoise's flat, although she graciously offered me her bed along with an elaborate story about why she wasn't using it anyway, because she normally slept in the spare room. I loved the digs, except for the lack of appliances. There was no dishwasher in the kitchen, and the bath-room housed a tiny clothes washer, even smaller than American "apartment-sized" ones. There was no clothes dryer at all—Françoise used a collapsible drying rack in the kitchen.

This was not a surprise, because the Parisian apart-ment I'd stayed in the week before had acquainted me with two odd contraptions. Tucked under the bathroom sink was a tiny washer-dryer combo that held only a few pieces of clothing at a time, took at least four hours to run, and resulted in a tightly tangled, definitively wrinkled, half-dry mess that looked as though it had been removed from a torture chamber just in the nick of time.

The apartment's kitchen appliance was even stranger. It was an oven/dishwasher combination. Each section had its own small door. The two little compartments did not seem to be functionally related, but I would not have been surprised to find soap bubbles rising from our roasted chicken.

Back to Françoise—she had spent time in America and was the perfect person to ask about differences between the two cultures. I broached the subject one evening in her cozy and romantic living room, where we were enjoying the wine and cheese—yes, really—we had picked up earlier in the day at the farmers' market, Françoise's favorite weekend haunt. Plants filled the room and candlelight threw flickering, jungley patterns on the walls. A CD of the neighbor's three-boy band provided fresh background music.

"Françoise, what do you think it is that makes a French woman French?" I began, expecting an articulate opinion on the tradition of powerful French women or the importance of a liberal arts education. Perhaps Françoise would tell me what it was like to live in a city that had been a cultural mecca for more than a thousand years. Maybe she would discuss the impact a confident and relaxed approach to sexuality—integrated into the culture—had on a woman's psyche.

But Françoise had her own agenda, and I had provided the opening. She wanted to know why Americans think the way they do about the French. "Why is it that whenever Americans use a French word, it has to do with only food or sex?" Françoise asked. "*Ménage à trois, rendezvous, soufflé ...*"

My Parisian friend had a point. I considered the "French" items that have become a part of our American lexicon: French cinema, French perfume, French ticklers, French dip sandwiches, French-cut green beans and my own favorite, French toast. Considering the fact that America is a nation of immigrants from around the world, the French *do* seem to have had an inordinate influence on the way we think about those two most basic needs, food and sex.

"It is as though you believe we live in a food and sex tunnel—but we are more than this!" Françoise protested. "We study occasionally. We work."

My review of "French" phrases did not turn up any that related to either study or work. (French horn? French bulldog? French cuffs?) The dearth was undeniable. But it got me thinking about French kissing—not a difficult topic to get me thinking about.

A few moments of consideration—not to mention the some-might-say *extensive* research I did in my late teens and early twenties—suggested that "French" kissing is surely universal, with the possible exception of the Inuit people, who, as everyone knows, rub noses in order to avoid the awkward situation in which a couple's mouths fuse together in the way-below-freezing temperatures of frigid arctic nights, and which can lead to both embarrassment and starvation.

Anthropologists say that about 90% of the world's cultures engage in the practice of kissing. I believe it is possible that some of the remaining 10% also engage in kissing, but prefer not to discuss it with their anthropologists.

Upon further thought, several pressing questions presented themselves: How do the French figure they can lay claim to a "French kiss"? What makes it French? Did the French themselves name it, or did some other nationality decide upon the moniker? And why is the practice so, shall we say, widespread?

Françoise explained that in France, a "French kiss" is a light peck on each cheek, a traditional greeting for friends of either sex—more akin to an "air kiss" than to a sexual act. The *other* kind of kiss is known as a *baiser amoureux* (lover's kiss) and in past times it was also referred to as a *baiser florentin* (Florentine kiss).

So the French attribute it to the Italians, specifically to the Florentines. But the Italians, along with pretty much everyone else in the world, attribute it to the French. In Czech it is *Francouzský polibek*, and in Turkish it's *Fransız öpücügü*. Chile, Nigeria and Austria apparently have similar phrases.

This research into French intimacies seemed promising, so I continued my quest at the Cadolle House of Lingerie, founded in 1887 by Herminie Cadolle, who is said to have invented the modern bra. Herminie first showed her new, two-piece undergarment—called *le bien-être* (the well-being)—at Paris' Great Exposition of 1900. It must have been a grand year for the structural engineering crowd; Gustave Eiffel introduced his tower at the same exposition.

Herminie Cadolle's renown as the inventor of the modern brassiere was recently usurped when an archaeologist authenticated a fifteenth-century bra found in an Austrian castle.

By 1905 the upper half of Herminie's invention was being sold separately as a *soutien-gorge* (literally "support for the throat," although *gorge* meant breast in old French). Bras are still referred to by that name in France, but Cadolle's were way, way out of my price range, so I opted instead to visit Sabbia Rosa, which my guidebook described as more affordable, yet "the underwear maker to some of the best-undressed mistresses in Paris."

Sabbia Rosa was too French for me. Although there were no other customers in the store, it took three shopkeepers huddled in the back a good five minutes of conversation before they deigned to greet me. The one who finally came forward was pushing seventy, had a fabulous body, and wore all-black clothing so tight I'm certain there was no room for even the slinkiest undergarment in there.

Her name was Louise, and she dripped gold and pearl jewelry. The only color Louise wore was an outrageously bold magenta lipstick. She showed me silk panties, string bikinis and flirty babydoll négligés. Then we moved to Sabbia Rosa's latest line: dainty floral-patterned silk camisoles priced between 380 and 600 Euros. Each. Fortunately, the designs were uninventive, and I was not even tempted.

But Louise was insistent. "These are all silk, all handmade, original designs."

"*Non, merci.*" I turned away.

Louise's magenta lips were on a roll. "You cannot find this anywhere else. You can wear for the day, for the night, anytime."

"They're out of my price range, but thanks for your time." I headed for the door.

"Mix with a party, wear with jeans; it is a concept!" Louise persevered, suddenly and surprisingly eager to sell me the silk originals.

I left Louise to her concepts, and returned to my own. My time in Paris was almost over, and I had learned very little of French women's secrets, except that they were probably expensive. Even if I had ransacked Françoise's lingerie drawer—a temptation I'm proud to report I resisted—I would not have discovered what makes a French woman French.

In a last-ditch effort to acquire some glimmer of French mystique, I popped into a department store and bought a slinky black camisole, cute undies and some gifts of French mustard to take home—that was as Parisian as I was going to get.

But how much could anyone expect to learn in a mere two-week trip? I will need to return to Paris to do more research—soon. And next time, I will not be intimidated by French women. After all, I have seen their household appliances. And I'm wearing their underwear.

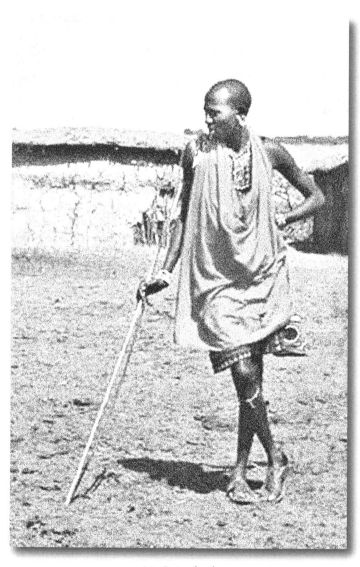

My Betrothed

MARRIED TO THE MAASAI
KENYA

Sweat slid down my neck in the midday sun and the powerful smell of cow manure assaulted my nostrils. I grew up in Iowa, where we raised cattle and referred to that odor as *The Smell of Money*. But in this Maasai village it was so overwhelming that I imagined microscopic scent-carrying particles floating through the air—rising up like angry insurgents from the dung-covered floor of the compound, traveling through shimmering waves of heat and swarms of flies, past little children's smiling faces, navigating their way through my nose hairs and deep into my lungs.

I am accustomed to stepping over the occasional cow pie out on the farm, but here in the village they covered the earth like a three-dimensional carpet. Perhaps I should have been appreciating all the signs of wealth littering the ground. Instead I silently cursed Victoria, my delightful Kenyan guide, for the devastating diseases I was surely acquiring. I'd have been cursing her aloud if I'd known then how the day would end.

Along with a dozen other travelers, I was touring a

village in Kenya—a *manata*—home to an extended family of about eighty people: a chief and his wives, their children and grandchildren, plus quite a few brothers, unmarried sisters, young cousins, and women from other tribes who had married into the family. Dixon, our Maasai host, was a son of the chief. He had brought sixteen of his brothers and cousins to greet us and show us around the village.

Most of the Maasai who lived here knew only a smattering of English, but Victoria, an outsider, spoke well. I loved Victoria's voice: a melodious tone with British inflections, quite beautiful in itself, but even more so because it was reassuringly familiar here in a place where I didn't speak the language, where all the men were warriors and wrapped themselves in swaths of cardinal-colored cloth, and the dry, treeless savannah stretched out for miles under an unforgiving sun.

Victoria wore a crisp white blouse and a navy skirt, befitting her position as an officially licensed guide. Her low-heeled navy pumps seemed impervious to the cow chips. "We will visit the manata and see the homes inside," she explained, navigating with effortless precision. "You'll learn about Maasai culture and have an opportunity to see the beautiful beadwork made by the women of this manata." Our visit would also include a performance of the spectacular traditional dances for which the Maasai are famous. "These men are warriors," Victoria proclaimed. "Dancing is not for the faint-hearted."

Maasai culture revolves around cattle, and Victoria peppered us with examples. "It is the men's responsibility to herd cattle during the day. The Maasai diet consists of cow blood and milk, supplemented by wild herbs. A Maasai man's wealth is measured by the number of cattle he owns. The penalty for murder is forty-nine cattle. Brides are bought with cattle and families are identified by the color of their cattle."

Dixon was at my side. "I am the son of the red cows," he said proudly.

I could identify with the importance of cattle—it is not so different from our culture, if you think of cattle as money. But there was another part of Maasai culture I could not comprehend—the emphasis on pain. When a boy is between five and eight years old, his two lower middle teeth are knocked out. If the teeth do not come out completely, the roots are dug out with a knife. Throughout this excruciating procedure, the boy must not scream or cry; he must endure stoically. If he does well, Dixon mentioned, "One of your uncles will definitely give you a cow."

A few years after that comes another ceremony, in which the boy's ear is pierced with a hot metal rod. Over time, progressively larger sticks are inserted into the resulting hole. This extremely painful procedure is done in the service of beauty, so men can wear large beaded ornaments in their ears. I began to think a little differently about my own culture's beautification practices.

Victoria explained that both the tooth ceremony and the ear piercing are done in part as "preparation for painful events in life." As I was wondering what events required such formidable preparation, she began to describe the Maasai's elaborate circumcision ceremony, which welcomes fourteen-year-old boys and girls into adulthood.

The teenagers participate eagerly, Victoria assured us, so they may take their place in the community, marry, and have children. A person who failed to participate would be outcast; her only hope for survival would entail a journey of several hundred miles on foot to the city, followed by a life of crime or prostitution. This seemed outrageous until I remembered that in our own culture baby boys are frequently circumcised as a matter of course. My perspective shifted again.

We walked towards Dixon's house, the one we were to tour. All around us sat traditional homes built from sturdy sticks and covered with thick cow dung, low and windowless like giant loaves of dark bread. The structures last about six years before termites make them uninhabitable. Then the whole village packs up, moves to another location, and rebuilds the compound.

I assumed Dixon's home was one of the extended family's nicer dwellings. At 5'3" I am a good foot

shorter than most Maasai adults; still, I had to stoop
down to enter, and managed to bump my forehead
on the header. The doorway was so narrow my
shoulders rubbed hard against the rough support sticks
on each side.

Inside it was dark and airless, and a heavy layer of
smoke burned my eyes. There were two rooms. The
first was empty of furnishings; it was where the
family's calves slept at night, protected from cold
winds and predators. The second room—the one for
people—was nearly filled by two sleeping areas, each
about the size of a double bed. They were separated
from one another by a shallow ditch in the dirt
floor. One area was for the parents and the other was
shared by all four of the household's children. Each
sleeping area contained only one thing: a "bed" consisting of a pile of sticks about two feet high covered
with a stiff cowhide. There were no pillows or blankets.
The remaining area held a hearth with enough room
for five or six people to squat around its small fire. A
cooking pot, one spoon and three metal cups completed
the furnishings.

We were told Maasai men must build the stick fence
around the compound—once every six years—and
herd cattle. The women of the manata are responsible
for everything else: milking cows, cooking, fetching
water from the stream that is nearly a mile away, wash-
ing clothes, building and repairing houses, gathering

wood and dung to fuel their cooking fires, caring for children and teaching them, and making finely crafted beaded jewelry for the family and for sale to tourists.

When I wondered aloud why the women put up with such inequity, Dixon explained simply, "In my culture the men are favored, more than the ladies." I was about to comment that Americans would never put up with such inequities, but then it occurred to me that we do.

After we learned about local customs and toured Dixon's house, it was time for traditional dancing. Maasai warriors are well known for their fierce dances; we were in for a show! Seventeen young men—tall, dark, lean, and dressed in bright red garb—performed for us. The warriors wore beaded head-dresses and necklaces, belts and bracelets of all colors. Elaborate earrings adorned the large holes in their ear-lobes. Several men carried drums, and one of Dixon's cousins wore a two-foot-tall headdress crafted from the mane of a lion he had killed himself, with only a spear.

For the first performance, the men assembled in two snaking lines and moved toward our little group in a kind of exaggerated, slow motion skip, which they managed to make look exceedingly menacing. Their wild appearance and unsettling movements were accompanied by an odd vocalization—something between a loud chant and very heavy breathing. The men purposely danced directly toward us, snaking their lines to weave in and among our group, heading at individuals as though we were standing in precisely the place where they needed to be. We each moved aside to get out of their way and they repeated this aggressive positioning, dancing us out of our spots again and again, creating a confusion I assumed was integral to the production. It was intimidating, as Victoria had warned us.

The afternoon heat was dizzying, and I grew tired of the dancing. By now it was mostly bunny-hopping up and down. Impressively *high* bunny-hopping, but even so, I'd had enough. The warriors' aggressiveness was irritating. I decided not to move out of the way, and instead played chicken with several dancing-hopping-chanting warriors who miraculously managed to complete their number without running into me. I felt a shiver of satisfaction at having stood my ground.

For the final dance, the warriors switched from heavy breathing to gutteral chanting. There was extended loud and energetic jumping, a chaotic waving of spears, more jumping, and rapid repositioning. When the pandemonium was over I stood alone, surrounded by a tight circle of seventeen tall Maasai warriors. Each one brandished a long, sharp spear and stared fiercely—unblinkingly—at me.

The rest of my group wandered nonchalantly outside the circle: silent, distant, tourists from another world.

The chanting continued, urgent and unrelenting. I wondered whether these were the same spears the warriors killed lions with, and glanced out toward Victoria, hoping for a reassuring smile. But Victoria's face was solemn, perhaps even a little worried.

I began to worry, too. What did the warriors want with me? What did the ongoing chanting mean? Shouldn't they be finished by now? Were they going to jab me with those spears? Did they want to trade me for their cows?

The rest of my group backed further away, angling for good photo opportunities. They were not in a hurry. I wondered at what point, exactly, it would occur to them to rescue me. When the chanting stopped? When the spears were raised? When their camera batteries ran down? Maybe they couldn't even see the top of my head inside the tight circle of tall warriors, and didn't realize I needed help. *Please, please, please!* I thought desperately, willing my prayer to rise like the chanting and the dung-dust and the microscopic angry-insurgent disease particles. *Please let them rescue me before the cattle are exchanged!*

The incantations grew more emphatic as the warriors tightened their circle, closing in on me. Their voices were loud and I could clearly see where the two bottom center teeth had been knocked out of each of their mouths. Their long belts swung out and slapped my legs. The smells of dung and sweat, the noise and color, drums and whirling movement, beads and spears, the heat from their bodies—they were so close, and the spears were so sharp!—were overwhelming.

And that's when I heard our guide's voice, clear and strong above the confusion. "Well," Victoria remarked calmly to Dixon, "She's married now."

*The Ringaskiddy Sheela-na-Gig Wannabe,
with "No Real Attempt to Bend the Legs"*

SEARCHING FOR SHEELA-NA-GIG
COUNTY CORK, IRELAND

Sheela-na-Gig's invitation is fraught with danger. Our relationship began with my quick peek at a wildly pornographic image in Thomas Cahill's popular book, *How the Irish Saved Civilization*. An ancient goddess, Sheela is rendered symbolically, stripped of all but the essential features. She is naked, bald, and often breastless, and reaches both arms behind her legs, using her hands to spread her genitals wide open—as wide as a barn door—in exuberant invitation. There was no question in my mind about the figure's intended meaning. As soon as I saw her, I was transfixed.

Evolutionary biology is my calling; sex, transformation, and renewal are my religion. I knew I would have no peace until I found this wild and fearless female creatrix. But how would I locate the surviving Sheela figures? My guidebook didn't even mention them. Could I go around asking civilized folks on the streets of County Cork where to find an ancient erotic goddess?

"Do you have an image of Sheela-na-Gig?" I began at the Tourist Center in Kinsale, a charming seaside village known for its fine crafts, world-class cuisine, and yachting activities. The buildings in Kinsale are well kept and brightly painted, and many are decorated with baskets spilling over with purple petunias and crimson geraniums; they're accustomed to tourists here. "I see you have reproductions of old Celtic carvings."

Margaret, a young shopkeeper, regarded me curiously. "Gosh, I haven't thought about Sheela-na-Gig since I was a wee girl. She was a screaming woman, wasn't she?" Margaret pantomimed holding her mouth wide open from both sides.

Hmmm. Right position, wrong orifice.

"When the monks came and brought Christianity, they didn't like her. That's all I really remember."

Was Margaret just being polite, or did she really believe that Sheela-na-Gig was a screaming woman? Perhaps that was the way her genteel mother had described the goddess to a young and innocent girl. ("Yes, Maggie darling, she was screaming, and the monks didn't like her making all that racket. It was *so* unladylike.")

A second shopkeeper, twenty years older, stood nearby, shifting nervously from one foot to the other, and tittering with quiet embarrassment. "And what about you?" I asked, "Have you heard of Sheela-na-Gig?" Surely she knew about a goddess who had been worshipped throughout the British Isles for centuries.

"Oh, no!" the woman sputtered hurriedly. "I'm English. I haven't heard of her a'tall!" I asked around a bit more, buttonholing women in shops and on the street, but got nowhere. Either they had never heard of Sheela-na-Gig, or they weren't admitting to it.

Clearly, a new approach was in order.

I determined to ask Sister Eily, a retired nun we were visiting with. Sister Eily had grown up in Ireland, and ran off when she was only sixteen—with her father's reluctant permission—to Australia to join the Order of St. Joseph of the Sacred Heart. Here was another fearless woman. After many years of service to the church, Sister Eily had retired and returned home to County Cork. She wore street clothes, sensible shoes, and a big, white, furry vest she'd bought for fifteen Euro in a thrift shop. It made her look like a Yeti.

Indelicate though the question might be, I was certain Sister Eily would tell me the truth. After all, nuns—even retired ones, I'm sure—aren't allowed to lie. They are also tough as tires. The sister didn't even blink at my question, although the right side of her mouth did curl up in a small, sly smile. She replied with an Irish lilt, "Oh, very little is known about Sheela-na-Gig."

I waited.

"She's the fertility goddess. A woman would go back into the church after giving birth to give thanks to Sheela-na-Gig. She would go alone, or with a few female members of her clan, and go at a quiet time when no one else was there. My mother would have done this, with her mother and her sister. I always wondered, in my heart, why the father did not give thanks as well, since it was his child, too."

Sister Eily mused that giving thanks to a fertility goddess "isn't really part of the Christian tradition." She thought it had most likely been a holdover from pagan times, explaining that "pagans, like the rest of us, worship God the best way we know how."

I next inquired about Sheela at a pub, where a green-eyed waitress with tight jeans and an easy smile raised my hopes. "She's a fertility goddess," Irene said. "There are no fairy tales about Sheela-na-Gig, and I'm not surprised that many people you've spoken with haven't heard of her. The old ways are being forgotten, aren't they? You'll find a site in Ballyvourny, on N25 past Macroom. Go out to a rural area, and ask the old men; they'll know."

I was surprised at Irene's suggestion that I ask a man about Sheela-na-Gig, but the opportunity presented itself when I met Desmond O'Grady, one of Ireland's greatest living poets. And I couldn't resist.

Dr. O'Grady had not shaved that morning. His pale blue eyes were watery; his eloquent hands waxy. His hair was gray, wild and wiry. O'Grady wore a tattered red bandana around his neck; a wrinkled, sage green shirt; and crumpled, pale pink linen pants that looked as though they had been washed with the bandana. He had been, long ago, a secretary to Ezra Pound and a good friend of Samuel Beckett.

During lunch, O'Grady revealed an ambivalence toward the feminine, dispensing such wisdom as, "Women writers? Women are only supposed to write checks," and "Cairo is a slum, except for the sphinx and her inviting orifice." His candor was promising; O'Grady was clearly no stranger to the earthier side of life. What did he think of Sheela-na-Gig? I had to ask the question that was constantly on my mind, if not my lips.

O'Grady knew her, all right. He looked me straight in the eye and warned, "Stay away from Sheela-na-Gig; she's good for nothin' but trouble! She'll take you for everything you've got, and then she'll come back for more." Then he ordered salmon and chips and a Beamish, admonishing the waiter not to forget the chips.

"Have you ever actually met Sheela-na-Gig?" one of our party asked.

"Oh, yes!" the great poet whispered. "'O'Grady,' she said, "I'm tough, and I live on Tough Alley. The farther down you go, the tougher it gets, and I live at the last house.'"

But the last house on Tough Alley is not Sheela's only abode. She was once prominently positioned in medieval churches and castles throughout Ireland and beyond, even onto the continent. From Kirkwall Cathedral in the Orkney Islands to Tracton Abbey in the south of Ireland, from Killinaboy Church in the west to Royston Cave in the east, Sheela's image spread widely across the British Isles. In Dunnaman, Cavan, and Killua, prominent rib bones give her a skeletal appearance; the Brigit's Well figure at Castlemagner and the Crofton-on-Tees image look oddly like current depictions of space aliens.

In Caherelly, Sheela's vagina is as large as her breasts, and in Oaksey and Kilsarkan it is bigger than her head! Often Sheela's face is moronic; sometimes it is frightening. At times there is no face at all. But the Sheela-na-Gig figures have one thing in common: an invitation to the great and fertile darkness.

Especially in Ireland, which was slow to adopt Roman Catholicism, ancient pagan imagery was commonly incorporated into early Christian iconography. For example, the Ballyvourny figure, which sits above a window in St. Gobnait's Church, was regarded as an image of St. Gobnait, who was the same person as St. Brigit, who was a personification of the pre-Christian Brigit, goddess of light and literature. Since the Reformation, most of the Sheela figures have been lost, destroyed, or disfigured; those that remain are often hidden in out-of-the-way corners. But they can still be found, and I was determined to do so.

I asked Benny, our knowledgeable guide, whether there were any Sheela images in County Cork. Guides here, as in much of the rest of the world, have an extensive understanding and recall of history and folklore, and are required to pass lengthy, exhaustive exams before being licensed. Surely Benny would know.

"Yes," he responded slowly, and after some consideration. "I'm sure I've seen a Sheela image nearby, right over a doorway ... but I cannot remember where. Maybe you should check the museum."

Stella Cherry, a lean scholar with a dry sense of humor, is curator at the Cork Public Museum, and kindly consented to show me the two Sheela-na-Gig figures in the museum's collection. They were not on public display. "The Irish don't seem to care about the figures," Stella explained, "But Americans are crazy for them." Stella had written a monograph about Sheela-na-Gig in order to provide more information for the Sheela-seekers who besieged her with questions. She even fielded a visit from "an American Professor of Vaginal Imagery," visiting Ireland to do some postgraduate research. Oh, those whacky Americans.

Writing up the information presumably allowed Stella to send searchers—and researchers—off to view the figures in situ, rather than spending her already-busy days communing with Sheelas in storage. Stella handed me a copy of her article, *Sheela-na-Gigs from County Cork*, published in the *Journal of the Cork Historical and Archaeological Society*, and led me to a closet that housed a fuse box, a washbasin, multiple mops and brooms, cleaning supplies ... and, on the floor, two Sheela-na-Gigs. Stella left me alone with them.

Each figure is a *bas relief* about two feet long, and is depicted standing upright, with fairly straight legs. Both have straight left arms, and right arms that are slightly bent at the elbow. Neither figure has ears, hair, breasts, or rib bones.

The carving known as the Tracton Abbey Sheela is in white stone and has a heart-shaped head with large, deep-set eyes, a small or damaged nose, tiny mouth and narrow chin. The arms and hands do not touch or overlap the body. A deep indentation in the center of the figure, in stark and insistent contrast to the rest of the convex surface, represents the genitals. It is frightening.

The Ringaskiddy figure is carved in what appears to be golden sandstone. It has a large bald head with narrow-set eyes, a long nose, and a wide mouth with a Mona-Lisa smile. A long, slender torso leads to short legs in a pigeon-toed stance. The figure's hands rest aside its genitals, which are represented with a simple, prominent, vertical line. Ringaskiddy aroused in me a feeling of amused affection.

I admit, though, I was disappointed. The features were more difficult to discern than I had expected, and these two both lacked the explicit, manual reference to genitalia that most Sheelas include. In fact, Stella refers to the figures as a "wannabe Sheelas," since there is "no real attempt to bend the legs." Even so, I felt fortunate to be able to spend some time with them.

Scholars disagree about Sheela's significance. Some say she was believed to have the power to "turn the evil eye" and ward off enemy attacks, and for this reason was often placed on castle walls. Others suggest she was the Roman Catholic Church's way of communicating the evils of lust to a largely illiterate congregation, explaining her frequent residence in the remains of medieval churches. Still others insist she was a fertility goddess, beseeched by new brides and barren wives, prayed to by midwives and women in labor, and profusely thanked by blessed new mothers.

These explanations seem wanting. Surely the "good luck" idea is overly simplistic. As for the second option, Sheela is not attractive; rather, she is often frightening. She certainly represents something other than comely sexuality. And the fact that Sheela's breasts and buttocks are not emphasized—in fact, her breasts are usually missing entirely—differentiates Sheela-na-Gig from fertility figures. (Contrasting, for example, with the voluptuous pre-Columbian fertility goddesses.)

I prefer a fourth explanation: Sheela-na-Gig, like the Indian goddess Kali, represents the devouring mother archetype—the source of life, death, and regeneration. She is "womb as tomb," the great mother whose capacity for destruction is requisite for the creation of new life. And her invitation, both terrifying and liberating, is nothing less than an opportunity to experience emotional death, transformation, and rebirth.

No wonder the images have been disfigured, hidden, and destroyed. They represent the feminine as the source of life, challenging the patriarchal father-as-creator perspective. Further, their symbolism embodies the unity of life and death, incorporating the "shadow" as essential to wholeness, rather than an evil to be overcome, or, at best, repressed. Little wonder, too, that the Sheela figures have attracted so many brave and crazy New-Age seekers, whose souls cannot bear the dissociative split of light from dark, and who ache for the powerful transformative process the Great Goddess promises.

As for me, I've found a touchstone, a vivid reminder of my own connectedness to the circle of life and death. And I'll be a regular visitor at the last house on Tough Alley.

*Cozy Trulli Home which I Wish was in my Own Back Yard,
but is Instead Located in Alberobello, Italy*

LEGENDS OF RESISTANCE
APULIA, ITALY

Apulia's rivers have run for millennia, but you cannot see them. Instead, pale yellow fields stretch out, dry and flat, criss-crossed by low stone fences. Sinuous ribbons of green vein the landscape; they are the only hint of an extensive system of underground rivers that escape the evaporative effects of heat and wind. Nevertheless, this narrow strip of land is productive: Apulia produces nearly half of Italy's olive oil, and about three-quarters of its fruits and vegetables. And, as I would learn during my nine-day visit, subterranean rivers are only the beginning of its surprises.

Strategically located between the Adriatic and Ionian Seas, Apulia was conquered by Greeks and Goths, Lombards and Byzantines. Its eastern-most town, Otranto, was infamously devastated by the Turks in 1480, on which occasion eight hundred prisoners were decapitated. But counterbalancing this history of oppression is a long tradition of creative resilience: As though they have taken advice from the earth beneath them, the people who live here have their own methods of overcoming seemingly indomitable circumstances.

Apulia is alive with history and legends of resistance, most notably the story of *trulli*. These charming homes are based on an ancient construction technique, brought to Italy by Anatolian tribes more than four thousand years ago. Once dry-stacked like the stone fences that surround them—and skillfully constructed using only locally available materials—*trulli* are testaments to their builders' ingenuity. Their grey conical rooftops sit like pointed hats atop whitewashed cylinders, stone circling upon stone with impressive precision. The *trulli* crouch in wide fields or huddle together to form towns like Alberobello.

And it was in Alberobello that I lived in a cozy *trullo*: one central room with a kitchen alcove, a second room with a bed, and a small separate bathroom. The walls, which were nearly three feet thick, kept the interior comfortable even in Apulia's hot summer, and also housed storage alcoves and cabinets. Above the main room was the rough wooden floor of a loft used for storage. A trapdoor in the kitchen provided access to the cistern. The front door, barely five feet high, was a constant reminder of times when people were smaller. I felt like a hobbit.

Trulli history gets interesting during the Middle Ages, with a law called the *Prammatica de Baronibus* that prohibited the construction of new cities without regal authorization—and taxation. Reluctant to share his wealth with the king, the local landlord, Gian

Girolamo II of Acquaviva—also known as *Il Guercio*, or "the man with a squint"—cleverly circumvented the ruling; he required that all construction in his fiefdom be done without mortar. That way, the dry-stacked *trulli* could easily be pulled down in the event of a royal inspection. Il Guercio thus avoided paying taxes, and at the same time pocketed money he collected from the resident farmers.

Neighboring feudal lords grew envious of the arrangement—such courtly jealousies were no doubt a common problem, back in the day—and brought a formal accusation against Il Guercio to the Royal Court of Naples. To avoid royal penalties, Il Guercio ordered the "temporary" *trulli* to be deconstructed, which, not surprisingly, angered the local citizenry who had been living in them.

Nevertheless, for many years hence the *trulli* were built, then disassembled to avoid taxes. Homes appeared and disappeared like mirages, until their inhabitants could bear it no longer. In 1797 they obtained an audience with King Ferdinando IV of Bourbon, who was sympathetic to their plight (or perhaps he was simply in need of additional revenues) and decreed that the town of Alberobello be freed from the Acquaviva family's control. Since that time, the *trulli* have been built with mortar—and the residents of Alberobello, one can imagine, have felt much more secure in their homes.

If *trulli* are the most obvious reminders of Apulian creativity, *pupi* are surely the most amusing, and the hilltop town of Grottaglie ("the original home of terra cotta") is the best place to find them. Here I wandered steep, winding streets spilling over with ceramics studios and shops. The shops, in turn, spilled over with *pupi*: ceramic figurines notable for their prominent, voluptuous breasts bursting out of tight bodices. If you visit, do not hesitate to examine them closely, for while *pupi* have the body of a woman, they may also have the visage of a man, including a luxuriant mustache! I couldn't help being charmed by such playful sexual ambiguity.

The tale of the *pupi* begins with the legend of *Ius Prima Nocte*, or "Law of the First Night," a medieval privilege—widely disputed by historians—that allowed the lord of a manor to deflower his peasant brides on their wedding nights. Once upon a time, a young man who was about to be wed objected so strenuously to this tradition that he determined to defy it.

Dressing up as a young woman, the man planned to impersonate his fiancée for the requisite performance with the lord of the manor. (The retelling did not address his specific plans for the actual confrontation. One would hope it was scheduled to take place on a dark, moonless night.) His costume was somewhat convincing, and the young-man-dressed-as-a-young-woman obtained an audience with the lord that evening, only to discover that he had made a small but serious error. In his haste, he had forgotten to shave off his mustache!

Now the lord was no fool, and even in the dark he quickly ascertained that the peasant in his bed was not a bride. The lord was so amused, however, by the young man's ingenious form of chivalry that he declined his *Prima Nocte* privilege, and they all lived happily ever after.

Grottaglie's ceramicists commemorate this historic event with the production of beautiful and skillfully made *pupi*, which have become a favorite souvenir for tourists and a source of income for the town. At the studio we visited, I asked a talented ceramicist, "The *pupi* breasts—are they inspired by your mama or your wife? Or perhaps by fantasy?"

"They are inspired," Leonardo answered with a wise smile, "by tradition."

Some Apulian traditions, however, are not so playful, as I discovered in Oria. Our guide there was Dottore Josepino "Pino" Malva, a compact man with pumpkin-colored pants, thousand-dollar Missioni eyeglasses and serious smoking habit. He held the keys to the private crypt—the one hidden beneath Oria's Cathedral Basilica—the one that houses a display of eleven mummified monks.

Italian mummies? These had not been mentioned on the itinerary. I had to wait nearly an hour to learn their story, during which time my thoughts wandered more than once to the Italians' fabled skill with fine leather.

First Dr. Malva guided us through the public areas of the cathedral complex, about which he was quite knowledgeable, having authored several books on Oria. When he finally led us to a blue door, painstakingly painted with a skull and crossbones, I knew the mummies could not be far. Several sets of keys later, we descended twenty-four narrow stone steps into the cool air of a crypt beneath the cathedral. I stopped at the doorway in stunned silence.

The narrow chamber stretched out before us. Along the left wall were eleven niches, each about five feet high and home to a mummified monk who would stand there for eternity—or at least for the indefinite future. On a ledge a few feet above them sat a long, neat row of more than sixty human skulls, cheekbone to cheekbone, each smiling up towards heaven. The scalloped symmetry of the skulls gave the row a lively, decorative feel, in contrast to the gruesome figures below. The room's only other adornment consisted of grey-on-black oil paintings of human skeletons in various states of work or conversation. One was shown shoveling a pile of skulls; another signing a contract.

Who had these men been, and why were their eerie remains preserved in the crypt? Plaques with names and dates of death told only a small part of the story. The earliest death was that of *Pietro Biasi, morto*

1781. In his mummified form, Pietro looks to the right; his right cheekbone is partially hidden by a dark shawl covering his head and shoulders, as though he has just turned his head. He appears to be calling out to someone. *Antonio Damico, morto 1825*, hunches his shoulders and clutches both hands over his abdomen, his face contorted as if in pain. The skull of *Angelo Oggiano, morto 1856*, is covered with a tattered black headscarf. He seems to have been caught in the middle of a macabre laugh.

These monks were members of the *Confraternity della Morte*, an organization not unlike the Knights Templar, which had the pope's official sanction to protect religious pilgrims on the road to Jerusalem. Members of the *Confraternity* believed it was a special honor to die in the military service of God, and a further honor, for both themselves and their families, for their bodies to be mummified so they could be venerated long after death. The order was therefore familiar with the process of mummification. But when Napoleon issued a decree forbidding burials inside church buildings throughout Europe, mummification acquired a new significance: that of a final act of defiance. If the monks could not be buried in the church, well then, they would be mummified and placed in a holy crypt instead. And so these warriors of God stand, grim reminders of another time. The *Confraternity della Morte* still exists, however, and is headquartered in Oria.

Exploring Alberobello, Grottaglie and Oria, I discovered that much in Apulia is not what it seems: the *trulli* were there, until they were not; the *pupi* are women, unless they are men; the monks could not be buried, and so, by God, they were mummified.

Stories create cultural continuity, passing along the characteristics that define a people from generation to generation. And these tales, of home building, wedding traditions, and even death, taught me about the profound resilience of the local people: Like the rivers that run beneath their fields, Apulians live life on their own terms.

Horse Meat Sold Here

Could I Eat a Horse?

ALBEROBELLO, ITALY

The instructions were unnerving: *Boil olive oil in a hot pan, lay the horsemeat in flat, and turn it when it starts to rise.* I tried hard not to visualize horseflesh rearing up out of a pan of boiling oil.

We were in search of the "Apulian delicacy" I had read about in a guidebook and was determined not to miss. My plan was to find a restaurant that served horsemeat, convince one of my more adventuresome traveling companions to order it, and then to beg the smallest bite, just a tiny taste—after all, it *was* a regional specialty. But things did not work out according to my plan.

I first asked at Casa Nova in Alberobello. It was a white-tablecloth restaurant with a large menu, and seemed a likely source. But I was met with a puzzled expression. *No*, they did not serve *carne de cavalle*.

Perhaps the waiter did not understand my broken Italian. "Horse, *cavalle*?" I repeated, pantomiming a gallop. I felt more than a little bit foolish pantomiming in a nice restaurant, but I was halfway around the world and really wanted to try horsemeat.

"No. No *cavalle*."

No matter; we still had more than a week to go. I would find it at the next restaurant. I persisted at Osteria degli Angeli in Lecci, at Ristorante Orsa Maggiore in Castro Marina and at La Sommita in Ostuni. Surely these fine Apulian establishments served the local specialty. But not a single one offered it. I tried requesting *carne equine*, thinking perhaps I had used the wrong word, but no matter how I asked, horsemeat was simply not on the menu. I enlisted the assistance of my travel companions: would they help me find a menu with horsemeat?

"Horsemeat?" Chrysa asked incredulously. "You want to eat *horsemeat*? Why?"

"It's a specialty of the region," I explained.

"I thought you were a vegetarian. How could you eat Mr. Ed?"

"I'm not completely. And I just want to try him. I mean *it*."

They promised to help look. Days passed, but no one found *cavalle*. (If I had not been looking myself, I would have doubted their sincerity.) Taking a seat one evening at La Cantina, I had nearly given up the search, when Connie and Linda spotted *Involtino al sugo di vitello o puledro* on the menu and alerted me from across the room.

Rolls of veal or horse and tomatoes, the translation read.

There it was.

In that moment, when I expected to feel delight, a seed of doubt arose. I was not certain whether I could actually eat an equine. I had never owned a horse; my personal experience of them was not unlike my experience of cows, visible chiefly in rural fields, and from a distance. I eat steak occasionally, but I began to worry that horses might somehow be different. Could I actually consume a Seabiscuit steak? A Black Beauty roast? Filet o' Flicka?

My companions were watching, waiting—probably thinking I would not go through with it. I ordered the *involtino*.

The waiter raised his eyebrow in what I took to be a disapproving look. Although horsemeat was listed on the menu, he informed me, La Cantina was not serving it tonight.

I began to wonder whether the dish really existed. Perhaps it was the Apulian equivalent of an urban legend, making for colorful copy in the guidebooks, teasing tourists, even appearing on the occasional menu, but never materializing in an actual meal. And perhaps that was just as well.

But Annelize assured me that horsemeat is indeed eaten in Europe: "It is common in France, where culinary appreciation surpasses sentimentality," she explained. This perspective momentarily renewed my resolve, as I am not accustomed to being accused of sentimentality.

"I ate it a lot as a student in Holland. It is very tender in comparison to the average beef," Annelize continued. "The muscle structure is somewhat coarser, the taste a little sweeter. I imagine it is comparable to human flesh; that is what cannibals report."

Cannibals? I did not like the direction this was heading!

The expression on my face must have matched my flagging enthusiasm, because later that evening Chrysa took it upon herself to assist in the quest. Since I'd had no success at restaurants, we switched to butcher shops. If they served the restaurant business, they would be able to tell us which restaurants to try. We located a butcher shop that sold beef, veal, goat, sheep, pork, chicken … everything, it seemed, except horsemeat.

"*Si vendono il carne de cavalle*? Do you sell horse-meat?"

"*Cavalle? No.*"

Did they know where we might find it?

"No."

We had better luck at a second butcher shop. Although they did not carry *cavalle*, they reluctantly sent us "down the hill, turn left, then turn right." We followed the directions, and ended up at a deli. No *cavalle*.

Chrysa persisted, searching up and down Alberobello's steep, narrow streets. Three hundred meters down the main road, Largo Martellotta, she saw the sign: *Macelleria Carne Equina.* (Surely the locals all knew it.) A second sign outside the shop featured a large horse's head.

Inside, Giovanni was sweeping up for the night. Not that there was anything to sweep; the store was spotless. All the meat had been put away for the evening; the empty glass cases and stainless steel counter sparkled. Gleaming white tile walls were sparsely decorated with framed photos of horses and donkeys. I was relieved that they had already closed.

"*Si vendono il carne de cavalle?*" Chrysa asked, poking her head through the open door.

"*Si.* Would you like some?" Giovanni pulled out a chunk of meat the size of … well, the size of a horse's head. It *wasn't* a head, of course. It was bright red and marbled with white, and it gave me the creeps. He cut us two thin steaks.

Our horsemeat cost less than 12 Euro per kilogram. Lamb was 20 per kilo in the butcher shop down the street, and veal was 22. Suddenly I understood why no one had wanted to serve me *cavalle*: it was budget food, most commonly eaten by students and others for whom price was a major consideration.

Giovanni showed us four pieces of paper, neatly stapled together. The first was a *Certificato Sanitario*, a health certificate pronouncing the meat *livero consumo*. My best guess at a translation was *freed for eating*.

I don't think the horse's liver was being singled out.

The remaining three papers documented Giovanni's purchase of the horse that had supplied our steaks, the name and address of the seller, our horse's name and birthday, the name of the ranch where it grew up, its parents, their bloodline, the date and place of the slaughter … the horse's upbringing and education, for all I know.

My resolve weakened.

Giovanni's wife, Dina, explained how to prepare the steaks. "Boil olive oil in a hot pan, lay the horsemeat in flat, and turn it when it starts to rise."

"Then what?"

"*Sale*, salt." Realizing that we were tourists and probably did not have our own supply of seasonings, Dina was kind enough to put a little salt into a plastic bag and send it home with us. A pinch of salt after we cooked it was all the steak needed, she explained.

Chrysa and I thanked Giovanni and Dina and left them to lock up the shop. We stopped at the deli to pick up a few other things for dinner, in case the horse-meat tasted awful. Back at our *trullo*, Chrysa fried the steaks according to Dina's instructions; they "rose" in the pan when cooked, just as she had said they would. I cut up fresh tomatoes and mozzarella. We rearranged some wildflowers Chrysa had gathered on her morning jog and set as pretty a table as we could. We wanted a pleasant ambiance for our first taste.

Chrysa was braver than I; she tried it first.

She liked it.

I swallowed my tomato and had a gulp of water before slicing off a piece of meat. I wasn't going to eat it with anything else; I wanted to really taste the horse. The first bite was moist and tender. It was delicious!

It tasted just like beef.

"Before" Shot of a Luwak and His Coffee Beans

MAGICAL BEANS

BALI, INDONESIA

It is the coffee I have come for—*the best in the world*. Buana Amertha Sari is situated on a tropical jungle road about halfway up the slope to Mt. Penelokan, near the ancient town of Bangli—once the capital of a Balinese kingdom. A wide pathway winds through the compound's gardens, lush with cocoa, papaya, pineapple, and pepper plants. And coffee.

Buana Amertha Sari produces world-famous luwak coffee—or *Kopi Luwak*, as it is known in Indonesia. Easily the most expensive cuppa in the world, its flavor is variously described as smooth, strong, extra-bitter, mild, almost syrupy, heavy with a caramel taste, without caramelization, with a hint of chocolate, with no bitter aftertaste, and/or lingering on the tongue with a long, clean aftertaste.

Such glowing-yet-confused characterizations make me suspicious that luwak coffee—purported to be the best in the world—is nothing more than a modern myth with a bungled marketing plan. But something in me wants to believe, just as people have always wanted to believe in a fountain of youth, in streets

101

paved with gold, in an ephemeral Shangri-La. I want this coffee to be rich and magical. *I want to taste the best in the world.*

Certainly what is most notable about luwak coffee is the subtle complexity that makes articulating its flavor almost impossible. Several university studies indicate that the number of flavor elements accessible in Kopi Luwak is about thirty percent greater than in regular coffee. That complexity—not the marketing —is why descriptions of luwak coffee vary so wildly.

Then there's the processing: Luwak coffee is so-named because it is made from coffee beans that have been eaten, partially digested, and excreted by a small Southeast Asian creature called the luwak. The raw beans, immediately after being expelled, are said to carry "the faint smell of stables you usually smell at a zoo." The price of these magical beans reportedly reached $1400 per pound in 2009, probably spurred by Jack Nicholson's eccentric predilection for Kopi Luwak in the movie, *The Bucket List.*

Kopi Luwak is not the world's only "naturally processed" coffee. *Kopi Muntjak* is made from the dung of the Southeast Asian barking deer *(Muntiacus muntjac)*, which also eats—then excretes—coffee beans. Muntjac are the oldest known deer, appearing in the fossil record some 35 million years ago, and are also of evolutionary interest because of their dramatic chromosomal variations: The female Indian muntjac has only six chromosomes. The Chinese muntjac, by way of comparison, has forty-six.

That was all I knew about luwak coffee when we

stopped at Buana Amertha Sari, but it was enough. Finding myself in its native habitat, I was eager to learn more about the luwak. Known to scientists as *Paradoxurus hermaphroditus*, and cousin to the mongoose, a luwak is stocky, grey in color, and about twenty inches long, with a tail extending another twenty inches. It sports a mask across its face and looks something like a cat or a raccoon, depending on your point of reference. (My own point of reference is the skunk, with which the luwak shares *the ability to excrete a noxious odor from prominent scent glands near its anus*.) Luwak coffee is sold as Weasel Coffee in the Philippines, and as Fox Coffee in Vietnam—where the luwak apparently resembles a fox.

But the elusive morphology of this money-making mammal is not *Paradoxurus hermaphroditus*' only paradox. I was intrigued by its species name, *hermaphroditus*. Does the luwak actually change from one sex to the other at some point in its life, like some animals do? (If so, what effect might this have on the flavor of the coffee?)

I was fascinated with the critter, eager to sample the coffee, and bubbling over with questions. Who had discovered that the excrement of a small nocturnal mammal could be scavenged from the forest floor, cleaned, and roasted to produce a superior cup of coffee? And how, exactly, was this discovery made?

The coffee is said to be exceptional because the wild luwak, having free rein of a coffee plantation, chooses to dine on only the ripest coffee cherries, in effect "hand picking" fine produce at the peak of its perfection. But is it really the luwak's choice of cherries that makes this coffee the best in the world? Or is it because of the beans' journey through the animal's digestive tract, where they begin to germinate and ferment, and enzymes seep in, breaking peptide bonds and freeing amino acids?

How does cage-raised luwak coffee compare the free-range variety? Can the flavor and aroma of beans from the droppings of a caged luwak ever match the deliciousness of those }gathered in the wild? Are caged luwaks fed anything other than ripe coffee cherries, and if not, do they move at a frantic, caffeinated pace? Also: How does one verify the authenticity of a brew marketed as the luwak's finest production?

The beans come out in clumps, retaining their shape and still coated with some of the fleshy berry's inner layers. They are carefully gathered from the forest floor before being exposed to the elements, especially rain, which can break them apart. The flavor-bearing nuggets must be delivered intact, since inspecting them is pretty much the only way a broker can ascertain that the coffee has indeed passed through a luwak.

I wasn't able to find the answers to all my questions, but I did learn that it was the avarice of colonists in the Dutch East Indies that led to the discovery of luwak coffee. In 1830, suffering both the loss of the Java War and the loss of Belgium, the Netherlands was on the verge of bankruptcy. Ever resourceful, the Dutch determined to speed their financial recovery by ex-ploiting Indonesian resources, so they instituted the era of *Cultuurstelsel*, which effectively prohibited native workers from picking coffee beans for their own use.

Observant Indonesians, toiling on plantations and thirsty for a taste of coffee themselves, noticed that the luwak consumed ripe, red coffee cherries, yet left the coffee seeds undigested in its droppings. The natives collected these cast-off seeds, then cleaned, roasted and ground them to make their own beverage. (It had not occurred to the colonists to criminalize this partic-ular hunting-and-gathering activity.)

The Dutch sampled luwak coffee and, recognizing excellence when they tasted it, began selling the luwak beans for an outrageously high price as long ago as the nineteenth century. In this way what had begun as an impoverished people's attempt—yes, I'll say it: their shitty little attempt—to use the meager resources they had available produced, in the end, the world's most exquisite non-alcoholic beverage. (This might be an opportune time to meditate on the rich headline pos-sibilities luwak coffee provides, from "The Straight Poop on Luwak Coffee" to "Good to the Last Dropping.")

I got a look at luwaks when I visited Buana Amertha Sari. Five cages, conveniently situated at eye-level amidst the gardens, house the famous mammals. I vis-ited during the daytime, and these little critters are nocturnal. Perhaps to others a luwak resembles a cat,

105

a weasel, a fox, or a raccoon, but the caged-and-slumbering variety looks like a small, nondescript ball of hair. I couldn't even see the animals' faces, which were tucked beneath other body parts* as they slept.

*It was here that I learned why their species name is *hermaphroditus*. Remember those *well developed scent glands near the anus?* They resemble exceptionally large testicles, and both sexes have them, prompting possibly-confused early researchers to call the animal *hermaphroditus*.

Exhausted from a long day of sightseeing, I welcomed the chance to relax, enjoy the view, and revive with a serving or two of caffeine. I took a seat at the cliff-side tasting salon, where a mild breeze cooled the humid afternoon. Steep green valley walls dropped into a white mist.

The Kopi Luwak Special was 60,000 *rupiah*, or about $6, which seemed quite reasonable for the best coffee in the world. It included one tiny pot of luwak coffee, plus a free tasting of six other house specialties, listed as Bali coffee Arabica, Bali coffee Robusta Female, Ginseng coffee, Hot cocoa Premium, Ginger tea, and Lemon Grass tea. I inhaled the intermingled aromas, rich and sharp.

It was time for a taste.

The Kopi Luwak would come first, of course. Would I be able to savor its *terroir*? What, exactly, would I be tasting *for*? *Musky* and *skunky* sprang immediately to mind; after that the possibilities quickly degenerated into even less appetizing adjectives. Perhaps I should focus on something else.

The best in the world.

I was about to taste the best coffee in the world. I emptied my mind of the details of luwak processing, and focused instead on the coffee's appearance.

Dark? Silky? Impenetrable? The best coffee in the world might be any of these, but my cup was none of them. It was almost watery-looking, for coffee. Definitely uninspiring.

The aroma, then? Fragrant, nutty, winey, spicy? Alas, the aroma, too, was unremarkable.

The provenance? No need to go *there*. Nothing was left but to taste the brew.

I had a sip.

It tasted like coffee. Smooth and mellow, a bit smoky, and—to my delight—providing not even a hint of its animal origins.

The Shangri-La of coffees?

The best in the world?

It's hard to say. But I offer this toast to the noble luwak, who surely experiences some uncomfortable moments in the service of coffee production:

> Here's to the luwak—
> That selfless fellow.
> Thanks to his magic
> My coffee's quite mellow!

Enthusiastic Italian Dining Companions at Alla Corta di Hyria,
Just After I Tasted the Figs in Balsamic Reduction

Waist-ing away in Apulia
APULIA, ITALY

To paraphrase a well-known aphorism, *a journey of one thousand excesses begins with a single bite*. And— one single bite after another—I happily ate my way through Apulia, in southern Italy. Anticipating the visit was a gastronomic adventure in itself. Apulia has a long coastline, an agricultural heritage and a tradition of frugality. It is known for healthful and unpretentious cuisine, influenced by centuries of interactions, whether by trade or invasion, with Greeks, Byzantines, Arabs, French and Spaniards. My heart was set on tasting the local specialties, particularly the superb seafood, *burrata* (a rich, fresh mozzarella) and *orecchiette* pasta. But my heart—and my waistline—expanded to embrace lowly vegetables, ripe fruit and humble bread as gourmet highlights. In Apulia, I discovered, fine food and folkways combine to make an irresistible repast.

Our culinary experiences, which I quickly came to regard as orgies of the very best kind, typically began between one and two o'clock in the afternoon and lasted until three-thirty or four, once even until five o'clock. As in many other countries, the long meal here is timed to coincide with the hot afternoon sun, which precludes heavy labor both indoors and out. But no matter what one's vocation, a meal in a hurry is an unthinkable insult in Italy, where sharing food is one of life's simple—and essential—pleasures. And the fact that the event was stretched out over such a long period of time somehow made my vacation gluttony seem almost acceptable.

We ate at least five courses at each meal, beginning with antipasti. These were typically five or six small, very flavorful dishes, such as mozzarella tied into a small knot *(nodino)* or fresh seafood. Often there would be julienned beets or carrots dressed with olive oil and vinegar. Ristorante Orsa Maggiore's antipasti included zucchini flowers fried in a light, tempura-like batter; and *pittule*, a fried croquette-like dish made with a batter of flour, potato and yeast surrounding a bit of blanched cauliflower. I never managed to choose among the antipasti. In fact, I felt compelled to try every one—in the name of culinary research—and a small bite never seemed to be quite enough. The antipasti were offered in such quantity and variety that I was inevitably satisfied after sampling them, but the main meal was yet to come.

After the antipasti we were presented with a "first course" of pasta and a "second course" of meat, the portions of which were inevitably generous and understandably quite filling. These were followed by

110

a palate-cleansing raw vegetable course at which slices of carrot, cucumber or *finocchio* (fennel bulb) might be served. At the restaurant Trullo d'Oro we cleared our palates with raw slices of a pale green, slightly sweet vegetable called *carocello*, specific to this region, which reminded me of a honeydew melon and others of a cucumber. Next came the fresh fruit course featuring sweet watermelon slices; perfect, firm-but-juicy Bing cherries; small, tart apricots and sweet plums during our June visit. We finished with cookies or a cake course and then a serving, if one dared, of frighteningly strong *limoncello* liqueur. An espresso was always available to top it off.

The meals were so huge and so delicious that I began to eat myself sick on a daily basis. And I began making promises to God: every day, I swore that if I could only finish this one last meal—sampling just a bite or two of everything that was offered—and then make it through the afternoon, I would never again overindulge. Every afternoon I pictured myself virtuously pushing away from the table at the *next* meal, maintaining my figure and my health. And every evening I sinned again, salivating the instant I saw the menu.

Mussels were among the most difficult to resist. Don Carmelo Ristorante Pizzeria served them in the peasant style—that is, combined with other ingredients into a one-dish meal, characteristic of this part of Italy because it was faster for working families both to

111

prepare and to consume. Preparing a mussel *tiella* (casserole) is quick and simple: Layer slices of zucchini and onion together in a baking pan. Add chunks of peeled potatoes, then arrange steamed, opened mussels in their shells on top. Add layers of rinsed rice and sliced tomatoes, and finish with Pecorino cheese and breadcrumbs. Bake in a hot oven for half an hour.

One taste and I became a mussel maniac. When cooked, the smooth, flesh-like morsels tightened and huddled—warm and peach-colored, sweet and tender—at the edge of their rough blue-black shells. They hunkered there, clinging, small and succulent, as if anticipating the approach of my hungry tongue and teeth. The mussels' slippery folds released trickles of the dish's rich juices, inviting exploration, and simultaneously providing plenty of selenium, vitamin B12, zinc and folate. I savored them at every opportunity.

Another local staple is *purea di fave* (broadbean puree). Many broadbean recipes call for the addition of cooked potatoes or a little milk for smoothness and to extend the dish. The heavy, pale puree is traditionally served with bread and a counterbalancing *cicorie*— wild chicory, salted and boiled, then cooked up with olive oil to a deep, bitter green. In the one-dish version, the chicory and fried cubes of dry bread called *cecamariti* ("husband-blinders") are stirred together with the bean puree.

The origin of the expression "husband-blinders" to

describe food is not clear. The most likely explanation, in my uninformed opinion, is that leftovers are used to create a dish so tasty that it dazzles—or blinds—a husband into thinking his wife has slaved for hours in the kitchen. But there is also the possibility the expression was used to describe a dish so filling it will placate a hungry husband, or a meal so delicious it will drive a husband to overeat, and subsequently to fall asleep. My favorite explanation suggests that *cecamariti* have the power of "putting husbands to bed, leaving wives free to meet their lovers."

Husband-blinding may be the most picaresque of Apulia's culinary traditions, but it is certainly not the only one. Fortified farmhouses—called *masseria*—dating from the sixteenth and seventeenth centuries dot the landscape. Inside, the *masseria* resembled agricultural factories: wheat was separated, grapes and olives were crushed, and cheese was made. Today, converted *masseria* continue their tradition as an important part of Italy's agritourism industry, providing intimate venues for weddings, cooking classes, romantic vacations and wellness spas. They still use house-grown or locally produced fruits and vegetables and often make their own wine, cheese and olive oil.

At Masseria Tenuta Pedale the fresh fruits and vegetables were irresistible. Here I discovered a delicious way to prepare carrots: *sott'olio* (under oil), parboiled and served with capers and a sprinkle of salt. Zucchini and eggplant are also traditionally prepared *sott'olio*: first they are salted and weighted to draw out moisture, then they are julienned, simmered with a little vinegar and water, cooled and dressed with garlic, mint and a drizzle of extra virgin olive oil. Trullo d'Oro in Alberobello served beetroots prepared in a similar fashion. I had expected balsamic vinegar or perhaps red wine vinegar, but in Apulia a simple white vinegar suffices.

At Trullo d'Oro I also enjoyed a perfect plate of *orecchiette* (little ears), another specialty of the region. These small pieces of pasta were traditionally made by local women, who pulled a bit of dough off a larger piece and used their forefingers to poke it into a "little ear," ideally shaped for catching and retaining sauces. My favorite way to eat *orecchiette* was with a sauce of hot fresh tomato chunks, a shaving of hard Pecorino cheese and fresh basil leaves. Something about this dish made me feel very naughty, as though I were actually chewing on the ears of little children, so I was tempted to hurry through it. But a perfectly *al dente* mouthful requires that one slow down and savor the flavors and textures.

La Cantina in Alberobello served one of the most irresistible culinary temptations: *burrata*, a local mozzarella that is simply, deliciously addictive. A large *burrata* is the size of an orange, a small one more like an egg. In fact, it reminds me of a soft-boiled egg, although round rather than oval in shape, with an outside layer the consistency of cooked egg white. Inside, a silky white melding of fresh mozzarella and cream bursts from its round white rind and spills forth like a soft-boiled yolk, oozing onto the plate, running together with the pool of golden olive oil that sits beneath the cheese. The taste is as creamy as one would expect, yet light enough that I could eat quite a lot—and I did.

Luckily for cheese lovers like myself, the companionably hearty Pugliese bread was served everywhere, its light, yeasty fragrance wafting from each restaurant table. Loaves have been made in the same way for centuries, and are deservedly world famous. Legend has it that the Roman poet Horace described them in 37 BCE as "by far the best bread to be had, so good that the wise traveler takes a supply of it for his onward journey."

Traditionally, Pugliese bread was baked into large loaves with an exceptionally crunchy crust for a long shelf life—easy to send off with a working husband who might be fishing or herding sheep for days or weeks at a time. Dense and pale straw-colored, its ingredients are hard wheat flour, water, salt and *biga*, a yeasted starter. Multiple long rise cycles and baking at gradually decreasing temperatures are the secrets to producing the chewy loaf; spritzing with water as it bakes produces the characteristic crust. Pugliese bread is even useful when stale; it is porous enough to absorb other ingredients and therefore ideal for making *crostini* and *bruschetta*, lightly toasted bread slices spread with olive oil, cheese, tomato, meat sauce or other savory toppings. And of course it is essential for the infamous *cecamariti*.

Good as Pugliese bread is, Il Gioiello (The Jewel) in Alberobello has improved it. Their version, dotted with crunchy almonds and liberally studded with chunks of dried fig—ripe, sweet and moist—served steaming hot, is the most delicious bread I have ever tasted. It was served with a sampling of fig jam, onion marmalade, and *marmellata di peperoncino e cioccolato*—a remarkable conserve of rich, dark chocolate spiced up with hot peppers. As I perused the menu, I made a mental note to follow Horace's advice and stock up on a few loaves for my onward journey.

And the figs! In Oria, Alla Corta di Hyria's figs with balsamic reduction were so succulent they inspired me to a *When Harry Met Sally*-like dining performance. Warm sweet fig halves slid into my mouth like oysters; their soft, furry skin a welcome surprise. Eyes closed, head tilted back, I settled into a moment of gustatory ecstasy, the fig's firm roundness heavy on my tongue, until the sweet-sharp tang of a sugared balsamic reduction filled my mouth and returned me to consciousness. Which was a good thing, because I would not have wanted to miss what came next: the rich, earthy flavors of *crostini con crema di tartufo*—rounds of crunchy toast topped with creamy truffle spread.

L'Ancora (The Anchor) in Monopoli served one of our finest meals, a two-and-a-half hour festival that began with a surprisingly tender little octopus. One bite followed another as we moved to what may well have been the most exquisite dish of our visit: lobster-drenched spaghetti. The silky sauce was deep adobe in color, thick and bisque-like, intensely flavored with lobster and peppered with small pieces of the sweet seafood. Ironically, this is the one dish I had tasted at home. Or perhaps it is not a coincidence at all that one of the finest recipes of the region should have been appropriated. In an attempt to recreate the meal in my own kitchen, I googled "recipe for spaghetti with lobster sauce" and got 156,000 results. If only I knew which recipe L'Ancora used.

But my final large meal in Alberobello was by far the most memorable. Bepe, a docent in the olive oil museum, invited me to his family's home in a multi-domed *trulli* in the countryside beyond Alberobello. Outside, olive and almond trees circled the house and huge, pink-blooming hydrangea brightened the front yard. Inside, a gay multicolored tablecloth peeked out from beneath more than a dozen dishes Bepe's mother had prepared for her family, the in-laws and cousins who lived next door, their grandfather and ourselves. I surreptitiously undid the button at my waistline and settled in for the feast.

The locally caught octopus was tender, light and

delicious. Cold, thin slices of beef served with a smooth sauce of mayonnaise and tuna were equally appealing. A cool *insalata di riso* (rice salad) proved perfect for the hot day: Pieces of tuna and sausage provided protein, and the light dressing of lemon juice and olive oil with capers added enough sharpness to balance the flavor. Bepe's family shared anchovies and omelets, salad, bread, olives, cucumber, pizza, cheeses and more. Then we moved outside for fruit, two cakes, gelato and *limoncello*. Not speaking Italian, I missed much of the conversation, but the hospitality was unmistakable. As my journey of one thousand excesses drew to a close, another maxim twisted in my imagination: *A waist is a terrible thing to mind.*

Grandma Hayes's Brown Soda Bread, Which is Almost Never Around Long Enough for a Photo, Because it is So Delicious

AN IRISH TRINITY

DUBLIN and COUNTY CORK, IRELAND

Long before we tackled yeast and its mysterious asexual reproduction, I learned to bake brown soda bread from my Grandma Hayes. She stood nearly five feet tall, always straight and proud, had red hair and freckles that she hated, and strong, cool arms that I loved. I didn't realize it at the time, but Grandma also taught me about transformation: creating rich sustenance from the simplest of ingredients. Brown bread always reminds me of Grandma Hayes. A loaf of it requires whole wheat flour, sour milk, soda, a strong stirring arm, and not a whole lot more. A slice provides nourishment and comfort beyond compare.

Thirty-five years after my grandmother's death, I visited Ireland's County Cork, a land of rolling green hills and patchwork fields—much like the farmland in southern Iowa where my grandparents settled and I grew up—and was stunned to discover Grandma's brown bread in nearly every pub and restaurant in Cork. Many of these establishments guarded their recipes for it fiercely. I know, because I asked for it at pubs like the Overdraught, the Armada, and the Mizen

Head. They all served brown bread, along with another dark substance I quickly learned to love—beer, and by beer, I mean Guinness and Beamish and Murphy's.

I drink beer now. Dark beer. A pint at a time, and it needn't even be cold. My favorite is Murphy's, a light-weight among dark beers perhaps, but with quite a respectable bite. First I down the head—a dense, creamy layer that tickles my nose and situates itself staunchly on my upper lip, neither dripping nor evaporating like the foamy froth on American beer. Instead, it makes itself quite at home until I dare to wipe it away. Sometimes I do not bother. The brew itself has a quiet silkiness, artfully balanced by a sharp and toasty bite that fills the mouth and quenches the soul.

I think I could live on Irish beer and brown bread, so I decided to search out the best. At the Guinness brewery in Dublin I learned how stout is made with barley, hops, water, and yeast. First, the barley is soaked in water, drained, and allowed to germinate. The resulting "malt" is roasted like coffee beans until it turns toasty brown; this gives the brew a rich, distinctive color and flavor. Hops are added for bitterness and aroma; then this concoction is mixed with pure, soft water and boiled. Next comes yeast, a rich source of protein and vitamins. This is where the asexual reproduction comes in. After it is added the brew is held in darkness for several weeks to ferment—the yeast transforming barley sugar into carbon dioxide (carbonation) and alcohol—and so the beer's flavor can develop and mature.

That was an easy lesson. Local brown bread recipes proved harder to pin down. At the Bride View Bar, Ann Marie, a fresh-faced lass with curly blond hair and a crisp white linen blouse, pleasantly refused to give away her brown bread recipe. She did divulge—in a conspiratorial whisper—that she uses a secret ingredient, and that it is *not* the cornmeal I had suspected. Gaby, our gracious proprietress at the Bellevue Bed & Breakfast in Baile an Cuainin confided that she includes treacle (syrup) and black walnuts in hers.

The short, round hostess at Jim Edwards' restaurant declined to give me her recipe, but cheerfully consented to explain the subtleties and secrets of *other people's* brown bread: "Some add an egg, some use sugar, white or brown, or extra treacle for more sweetness; some prefer sour milk over buttermilk; and be certain to sift the soda! If you line the loaf pan with buttered parchment, it will ensure that the crust stays moist, and the bread will last four or five days, rather than the usual one or two."

After my diligent investigation of brown bread and beer, I thought I understood a good portion of Ireland's rich, dark culinary heritage, but Gaby had one more surprise for me: a breakfast of Clonakilty black pudding. Although it isn't really pudding, it *is* really black, and it is served in soft, sausage-like discs, each about an inch and a half in diameter and three-eighths of an inch thick, regularly studded with pale kernels of what turned out to be barley. The kernels had just enough bite that they each popped—a bit like caviar—under the tooth, after which the pudding was bulky enough to fill the mouth roundly, with a rich creaminess.

The whole of it was perfectly seasoned, salty enough to compel another bite, and with just a tease of pepper, that came onto the tip of my tongue well after I had swallowed the rest, each morsel suggesting that another mouthful might very well be in order. What ultimately seduced me was the generous texture—the gentle pop, a creamy chew, and only then the peppery suggestion. This could easily become my favorite food, except for the fact of what it is: Blood.

The *black* in black pudding is congealed pork blood, and I am nearly a vegetarian. So I nibbled at the stuff excruciatingly slowly, considering with each small bite—and in between bites, too—exactly *what* I was eating, and straining to taste an excuse to push the plate aside. The excuse never manifested; Clonakilty's black pudding is, in fact, delicious beyond description—a perfect comfort food.

And comfort has long been needed in Ireland. After all, it is a country whose inhabitants have endured no small amount of hardship. I have often wondered about the mystery of Irish authors—Swift, Wilde, Joyce, Beckett, O'Brien, and Doyle, to name a few greats—how these people, who have been invaded and oppressed for centuries, manage to produce such lyric laments. How do they create pleasure and nourishment from such a bitter history? Perhaps the darkness of their subjugation allowed pain to ferment into music, and longing to transmute itself into poetry. Is it not so different from yeast, rising in darkness from a single cell to form a rich source of sustenance?

Yeast was in Grandma Hayes' larder, and Yeats was in her library. I learned both their lessons well: In "Cuchulain's Fight with the Sea" Yeats seems to reveal some of the mystery behind Ireland's mystical transmutations.

> *I only ask what way my journey lies*
> *For He who made you bitter made you wise.*

Wise indeed—in bread, in beer, in blood—an Irish trinity worth toasting.

Is there anything better than sharing your favorite comfort food with friends? Here's my grandmother's recipe. Enjoy!

Grandma Hayes's Brown Bread

2 cups sour milk*
½ cup sugar
½ cup sorghum or dark molasses
2 tsp soda
1 tsp salt
1 cup white flour
2 cups graham flour

Combine milk, sugar, and sorghum. Sift together and stir in soda, salt, and white flour. Stir in graham flour and pour into a greased loaf pan.

Bake at 350° for one hour.

*Or put 1 Tbsp vinegar into a 2-cup measuring cup, then fill it up with regular milk. It will sour and thicken.

Entrance to The Great Mosque of Paris, Which I Did Not Visit
Due to an Impending Demonstration

Bien-Être at the Hammam
PARIS, FRANCE

I pried open the small plastic container and slathered my wet body with its contents, which looked and smelled like an under-refined petroleum product. The goop may have been mildly herbally infused, and perhaps it was some-what amber in color, but the resemblance to a blob of sticky brown petroleum jelly was unmistakable. I stood frozen this way for a moment— nearly naked, smeared with goop—in a room full of strangers who did not speak English.

Was this really the way I wanted to spend my last afternoon in Paris? I replayed the events that had brought me to such an odd and vulnerable position.

"You should treat yourself and go to a *hammam* while you are in Paris," Marie had suggested, her eyes twinkling. Marie, a good friend of a good friend, had met me at the Luxembourg Gardens for afternoon tea, and was suggesting typically Parisian activities for the rest of my visit. I liked Marie and instinctively trusted her judgment, but I had no idea what a *hammam* was, or whether it would even remotely resemble my idea of an enjoyable activity. It sounded exotic and vaguely dangerous.

"Do you think it is safe?" I asked.

"Yes—and it is very important not to be frightened by all these protestors. There was a time in Paris when there were terrorist activities every week, but we continued with our lives."

Despite Marie's emphatic admonitions, this did not sound like a promising way to spend an afternoon. She was referring to a protest that had been scheduled for the following day at the Great Mosque of Paris, founded in 1926 in a grand gesture of gratitude to the 100,000 French Muslims who died fighting against Germany in World War I. It is said that the Great Mosque also played an important role in providing sanctuary and refuge to Jews during the Holocaust.

The protest was in response to the anti-Islam film, *Innocence of Muslims*, and subsequent cartoons mocking the prophet Muhammad in the Paris-based satirical magazine *Charlie Hebdo*. France's prime minister, Jean-Marc Ayrault, had just announced a ban on the protest, since worldwide demonstrations had resulted in more than one hundred deaths in the past ten days.

"These activities will not affect you anyway," Marie predicted, negating the terrorist threat with typically Parisian efficiency.

I still needed to figure out what a *hammam* was, so I looked it up online: "Both women and men in North Africa and Turkey have long enjoyed the ritual steam bath or *hammam*: a term which now designates not only the hot steam room itself, but the haven of calm that also generally includes a dimly lit room filled with cushions where you can take a nap or sip mint tea after bathing. In part due to France's former colonial presence in North Africa, the *hammam* tradition has since become a staple of French urban *bien être* (well-being)."

It sounded fabulous. This would be my defining Parisian experience. My two weeks in the City of Light were nearly over, and I longed to wrap up the trip with an indelible event—plus, I was ready for some pampering.

True, I had already enjoyed a "haven of calm" in the soaring, light-filled, hush-toned Louvre (except for the half-hour when I was lost, and a little panicky, in its vast expanses); in the lush, dim, golden-hued Tea Room at the ultra-posh Hotel Meurice (aside from the part about getting kicked out for shooting a photo— *one photo*—inside); and in the relaxing gardens of the Jardin des Plantes, which were so inviting that I indulged my jet lag and took a short nap on the lawn (shorter than I would have liked, because the garden police interrupted it almost immediately).

As it happened, one of Paris's finest and most authentic *hammams* was a short walk from the 19th *arrondissement* apartment where I was couch-surfing with another good friend of a good friend. My host, Françoise, also encouraged me to go. "I've been to the *hammam* at the Grande Mosquée de Paris, and it was very relaxing, but you should not go there now because of the protests that are scheduled. The *hammam* here in the 19th will be much better," she said.

"Do you think it is safe?"

"Oh yes," Françoise insisted. "The people at the *hammam* are very tolerant and welcoming. You will not have any problems out here."

I hesitated. What if there was a demonstration at this *hammam*, located in a student-filled, not-exactly-upscale neighborhood in which conservative—and separatist—Jews and Muslims lived? Being caught in the middle of a protest that was likely to turn violent was definitely not my idea of a relaxing afternoon—especially in a country in which I was politically naive, and didn't even speak the language. The only thing worse would be *being caught naked, in a room full of swirling steam, without my glasses*, in the middle of a protest that was likely to turn violent in a country in which I was politically naive and didn't even speak the language.

That was the stuff of nightmares.

I decided to go anyway, however, because I trusted Françoise. She had been a delightful host and was becoming a good friend. If Marie and Françoise both said it was safe, I believed it would be safe. If they said it was relaxing, I believed it would be relaxing. And if they were wrong? Well, if they were both wrong, I could be in big trouble.

I headed over to the *hammam* at four o'clock on a Sunday afternoon. The website said Sundays were women-only days, differentiating them from Saturdays, which were open to both men and women ("bathing suits required"). Given that distinction, and the fact that neither Marie nor Françoise had mentioned a bathing suit, I could be forgiven for having inferred that I did not need to bring one along on a Sunday.

I entered and pronounced the only French I knew: "*Excusez-moi. Je ne parle pas du Français. Parlez-vous Anglais, s'il vous plaît?* Excuse me. I do not speak the French. Do you speak English, please?"

As three attendants scattered in search of the one person on the premises who spoke a bit of English, I took in my surroundings. Elaborate blue and white geometric tile-work crept up the walls, punctuated by occasional squares of watery aquamarine. Gold and crystal chandeliers sparkled overhead. To my left, a small group of women enjoyed tea and pastries in a dimly lit room lined with low, sumptuously cushioned banquettes.

A tiny woman—with a nametag that said *Leila*—emerged to assist, handed me a locker key, and led me into the changing room. "Do you have ..." Leila gestured toward my pants.

Seeing that the other women in the room, in various stages of undress, were equipped with bathing suits, I shook my head *no*. "OK. It is no problem." Leila left and returned almost immediately with a pair of bright red bikini bottoms, which turned out to fit me perfectly.

But what about my top? The other women were wearing two-piece bikinis *with tops*. My friendly little attendant handed over a large, plastic-wrapped stack of supplies, consisting of a white terrycloth robe, a large towel, a small towel, a patterned *pareo*, plastic sandals, a plastic cup filled with brown goop, and a rough-textured blue mitt that closely resembled the scratchy thing I use at home to clean exceptionally stubborn pots and pans.

Overestimating my intellectual capacity, Leila quickly explained the entire process using a little English and a lot of pantomime: I was to change into the bikini bottom; don the robe; create a secret four-digit locker number and close the locker; descend to the shower room; hand my key to one of six exfoliation specialists; massage the goop onto all of my body except my face and feet (she said *just* my face and feet, but I figured out what she meant); enjoy the steam room and dry sauna; remember to shower before the cold pool; *Yes*, there was time for the exfoliating scrub but *No*, I could not have a massage because the *hammam* was very busy that evening, and at six o'clock I could have a facial, which consisted of massage, a "treatment," and something that sounded like *black skin*.

So far, I was not experiencing the haven of calm. In

fact, I was feeling confused and a bit anxious. Not to mention underdressed.

There was no mention of the *pareo* or the blue mitt, and it was not clear whether I was to carry my stack of supplies along to the steam room or leave them upstairs in my locker. Leila took everything but the goop, directed me toward the shower, and disappeared.

Well, this I could do. The room was warm and steamy, the shower was generous, and there were enough other topless women that I did not feel self-conscious. The "goop" turned out to be argan oil, a creamy luxury cosmetic that made my skin feel soft and nourished. The steam room enveloped me in heavy swirls of humidity that forced me to breathe slowly and shift my focus to the four-foot radius immediately around my body, which was as far as I could see.

Time slowed.
My mind wandered.
My body moved easily,
   flowed
    from steam room to sauna
   from slow shower to chair,
  steam room,
   nap by the pool
murmur of voices,
 unintelligible river

French
Arabic
shower
cool plunge
rush of current
lull of steam
sweat
haven of calm
yes ...
Haven of Calm.

I awoke at five-thirty in the afternoon, retrieved my scratchy blue mitt, and wandered over to one of the massage tables, where another attendant motioned for me to lie face down as she used the mitt to give me a vigorous rubdown. It felt like she was scrubbing my skin with sandpaper, except behind my knees, where it felt like she was scrubbing sunburned skin with sandpaper. I decided that next time I scour a pan at home, it would be nice to say a little apology to the pan, perhaps even to murmur aloud a small acknowledgment of what I was putting it through.

Next came a shower, a cold plunge and a facial. After I had dried and dressed, Leila led me to the tea room and brought out a glass of steaming, sweet mint tea, along with a dessert pastry filled with custard, almonds and honey. The pastry was small—only two bites. But they were *perfect* bites: flaky pastry, rich and creamy custard, crunchy almonds, pale honey dripping down the side. This was surely better than tea at the Meurice. Leila also retrieved the still-damp blue mitt, pantomiming that it was mine to keep.

On the walk back to Françoise's apartment, I gave thanks for Paris's peaceful immigrant population, for the soft evening air, and for friends of friends. The blue mitt now sits atop my kitchen sink, awaiting a suitably grungy pot—it might also be useful for refinishing furniture—and reminding me, every day, of my own personal Parisian Haven of Calm.

A Magical, if Somewhat Frightening, Face in Ubud

Eat, Pray, Scrub
UBUD, BALI

I don't normally swallow mysterious pills from strangers, but in Ubud I made an exception. This small-but-lively city is the health capital of Bali, and nearly every other shop offers massage, foot reflexology, spa services ("Be a Balinese Princess for a Day") or organic health drinks based on carrot, apple and papaya juices, with substantial infusions of ginger, mint, and lemon.

The strangest of these treatments is one in which you submerge your afflicted body part in a large aquarium—in public—and allow a school of tiny "doctor fish" to nibble away at dead skin cells, bacteria, and whatever else happens to be clinging to your personal ecosystem. This procedure is said to "regenerate" your skin. Word was going around town that a German tourist had recently submerged his entire head in a tank, in hopes of curing the psoriasis on his scalp.

But I had a different sort of health adventure in mind. Inspired by the Lonely Planet guidebook to Bali & Lombok, which devotes an entire page to "*Eat, Pray, Love* & Ubud," I couldn't resist tracking down one of the book's star characters, herbal healer Wayan Nuriasih, and trying her *jamu*—traditional Indonesian homemade medicinal concoctions.

I didn't really have any medical complaints, and had read that tourists eager to experience Balinese healing were crowding out natives with serious health problems, so I had mixed feelings about taking up a healer's time. But the Balinese recognize stress, worry, "busy minds," and "revitalizing weary spirits" as legitimate concerns, so I rationalized my curiosity. Besides, contributing to the local economy is part of my responsibility as a tourist, and this was more appealing than heading home with a suitcase full of souvenirs.

Wayan's health drink-serving, palm-reading, future-forecasting, vitamin-prescribing, herbal-scrubbing, massage-giving bodywork shop wasn't hard to find, even though its small sign was hidden in a tangle of half-dead bougainvillea. The establishment is tucked away on Jl Jembawan street, a narrow, motor scooter-clogged lane just off Ubud's main drag. Like many Balinese stores, this was an indoor-outdoor affair with no permanent front wall—a wise arrangement in such a hot and humid climate.

Inside, Pepto Bismol-pink walls displayed colorful textiles, red and gold patterned bunting, Hindu offering baskets, landscape paintings, an illustration of internal organs and chakras, portraits of minor deities, and a large photo of Elizabeth Gilbert—the *Eat, Pray, Love* author. Given the economic prosperity Gilbert's book has brought to Ubud, I wouldn't be surprised if she is now considered a minor deity. Two tables and three chairs, none matching, crowded the room. Papers, notebooks, incense sticks, stacks of fresh herbs, apothecary bottles, packets of tea, and colorful boxes of medications littered the tables. To the right stood a tiny kitchen, just large enough for preparing the health drinks. The entire front of the shop opened directly onto the street.

Lonely Planet's writers had warned me against the potential hazards of EPL healers: *You will be told a variation on the theme that you're smart, beautiful, sexy, and will live to 101 or 105 etc.... Note that it is important to have a very clear understanding of what you're agreeing to, as it's easy to commit to therapies that can cost US $50 or more.* I arrived at ten-thirty in the morning, hoping there would be plenty of time for the quickest (and least expensive) treatment before I met friends for lunch.

Two young Dutch girls—beautiful, blonde and tan—were ahead of me. Wayan counseled one about her future: "In your life you will have five men love you. Three big love, one small love." Mathematics was apparently not one of her strengths, but the girls didn't seem to mind.

Since no locals stopped by while I was there, I stopped worrying about monopolizing scarce healing resources.

Instead, I relaxed and enjoyed an exceptionally healthy tasting herbal drink while eavesdropping on Wayan and the Dutch girls. "You come from eight generation reincarnation. Sometimes three generation. Sometimes seven generation. You will have two boyfriend at one time."

The girls giggled. *"Yes, that could happen!"*

"Yes, two men will love you at same time," Wayan pronounced.

I decided I did not require a "future reading."

After she finished foretelling the Dutch girls' futures, Wayan—who stands about 5'3" with smooth light-coffee skin, glossy black hair, and full lips—turned to me. Her healer's uniform consisted of a thin T-shirt with a cartoon of a boy and girl holding hands and kissing, and the words *Spring Love* emblazoned in pink across the top, plus an Indonesian sarong and bright green ceremonial sash.

"You want treatment?"

I explained that I had come for the body reading only, the one that was listed on her menu board for 300,000 *rupia*, or about $34. Wayan directed me to fill out a form with my name, address, and date and place of birth. She recited that information aloud, said several short prayers, and burned incense in a traditional palm-leaf offering basket filled with marigold petals and a bit of rice.

She then asked me to stand and remove my accessories:

watch and earrings off. I worried, for just a whiff of a moment, that I would never see them again. Facing me, Wayan stood and lifted each of my hands so gently it felt as though they were floating, and examined both palms and my fingernails. She noted the lines on my right palm, making a quick sketch.

Next Wayan pulled down the skin in front of each of my eyes and studied the whites. She lifted my arms skyward and briefly raised my blouse up above my bra, then pulled it down again—this was in full view of the street. I began to wonder whether some aspect of my "body reading" involved entertaining the neighbors.

After I had finished flashing the folks walking along Jl Jembawan, the healer asked me to remove my sandals and place one foot on the chair in front of me. Then she felt my left knee and shin lightly, and pronounced that I had a hurt knee (I don't) and a bad memory. (Maybe I *did* have a hurt knee, but I forgot?)

In fact, Wayan recited a whole litany of problems I do not remember ever having been bothered by. It was a rapid-fire diagnosis:

Wayan: You have small gas, small bloating, yes?

Me: No.

Wayan paused.

Me: Well, maybe once in awhile. (It was a possibility. Perhaps I didn't need to lose that last ten pounds after all—I just needed to get rid of the "small bloat." I was beginning to like Wayan.)

Wayan: Does anyone in your family smoke?

Me: No.

Wayan: You have small smoke in your lungs. Do you take high blood pressure medication?

Me: No.

Wayan: Blood pressure low to medium. Don't eat so many eggs. Blood not so clean. Need better circulation. Vitamin E low: Eat seaweed, beansprouts. Calcium low: Eat broccoli, long beans. Skin dry: Eat water spinach. Bad bones lead to arthritis, symptoms already show!

On this count, Wayan may have been correct. I have, on at least five occasions in as many years, noticed a slight ache in my right pinky finger, which I now suspect might be an early symptom of arthritis. Wayan may have been right about the calcium, too; my doctor at home has been bugging me for years to take supplements. I've resisted, having heard on my favorite radio health show that our bodies tend to misappropriate non-food-based calcium supplements, depositing the mineral in joints and causing arthritis.

And the eggs ... I had been eating eggs for breakfast every day since arriving in Bali; definitely too many eggs. Maybe this was a lucky guess—Wayan surely knew that all the local hotels offered a complimentary omelet breakfast. On the other hand, it was possible that Wayan was indeed a talented medical intuitive. (My blood pressure is fine, and I do occasionally inhale secondhand smoke at parties.)

After the body reading, it was time for my future reading. When I declined—remembering the Dutch girls—Wayan suggested a rejuvenating massage. Was this the bait-and-switch Lonely Planet had warned against?

"Is it included in the treatment?"

"Yes, same 300,000 *rupia.*"

When Wayan handed me a gorgeous gold patterned sarong and told me to go upstairs and change, I was happy to comply.

The upper floor was even more cramped and chaotic than the entry level: several massage tables, a bed made of multiple thin mattresses pushed together, stacks of papers, reference books, and a desk covered with bottles of medicaments packed the room. Tall stacks of meticulously folded sarongs and clothing covered one whole wall; on another hung many framed certificates, including a massage therapy certification from Esalen.

In the middle of this chaos perched one of the blonde girls, half naked, and looking somewhat bewildered. I think she had also been sent up to change, but then forgotten.

I undressed, wrapped the sarong around myself, and descended. An assistant led me through the tiny kitchen, counter stacked high with drying mismatched dishes, and into a cramped room labeled *Toilet.* Indeed it was. A turquoise ceramic squat toilet was installed in the far corner, next to a plastic chair on which I was to sit. An acrylic painting of a large red rose blossomed lushly over the toilet.

I took my seat and rested my feet on a low stool that stuck out through the Toilet doorway. My view through that doorway of passersby on the street was excellent. Their view of me was no doubt entertaining. Two assistants began rubbing me vigorously with warm wet leaves, which quickly disintegrated to resemble soggy brown paper towels—the kind I associate with poorly maintained gas station restrooms.

The assistants, both exceptionally buff middle-aged men, brought to mind the "Kuta Cowboys" I'd heard work southern Bali beaches, servicing vacationing ladies of a certain age. This must be where those cowboys retired! One worked on my legs, the other on my neck and arms. Their scrubbing was so earnest and energetic that I began to think of exfoliation as an extreme sport. Wayan watched over the men closely, directing their work. I watched closely, too. Their tan, muscled forearms were impossible to ignore.

Wayan gave me a handful of the wet weeds and directed me to pull the front of my sarong out and rub my front with them, which I did. She also said, "Vagina bottom," which I did not. We were still in full view of the street. My desire for rejuvenation *does* have its limits.

She then handed me another bunch of herbs and told me to rub my face, "Like makeup. Stronger, stronger." She mimed rubbing under my eyes, and I followed her instructions a bit dubiously. I had always heard one was to treat the sensitive under-eye skin with the utmost delicacy.

Without warning, one cowboy dumped about a gallon of something cold, wet, and lemony-smelling over my head. It occurred to me that the spectacle of an unsuspecting tourist—naked, except for a flimsy cloth wrap—being suddenly doused with cold liquid was not unlike that in a carnival where spectators throw a ball at a target to plunge some poor clown into a tank of water.

Next, both cowboys rubbed me with coarse salt. "Herbal scrub will make your skin not too dry," Wayan promised. "You will see change immediately." My skin has always been soft; I felt a little insulted, and doubted whether Wayan and her cowboys could improve it.

"How will I maintain this renewed health at home?" I asked skeptically. After all, what good was rejuvenated circulation if it only lasted a few days?

"You cannot get, must live here. Herbs are from India, South America, China. Hard to get. You must come here. Come again tomorrow if you are not balanced." Then Wayan cracked herself up: "Come again tomorrow, pay again tomorrow!" she laughed.

The xeroxed healthcare handout I received cracked *me* up. It contained several unfortunate typos: "Medicine before Helling," and "Other medicine for take way in one Fakage."

Wayan produced a glass of hot water along with two capsules labeled "Calcium" and seven round hard globes that looked like gigantic brown peppercorns.

"Swallow these!"

The big round pills were Penenang, for "not busy mind," and they hurt going down. I also received a box of pills for "soft and beautiful skin," which I took as a good sign: Wayan hadn't prioritized my unclean blood, so maybe it wasn't that big a deal after all. And finally, I got two small packets of fresh gotu kola herb, to improve my memory. "It's all over Internet," Wayan explained. "You can look it up."

I thought we were finished, but Wayan declared my body was *not balance yet*. Although this seemed to be an extra treatment, I did not protest when she took me upstairs and indicated I was to lie on the massage table, face up, with my head on a small pillow. Wayan removed my sarong and began deep, firm massage on my belly with oil. Never have I been so thoroughly palpated—not even by my internist! When she had finished, Wayan swept a large red plastic rice spoon across my belly to remove the oil, and perhaps any toxins that might have been released in the massage process. She snapped the rice spoon with a practiced wrist at the end of each swipe. There was no extra charge for this additional balancing.

I retrieved my watch and earrings, dressed, and met

my friends for lunch. I did not feel rejuvenated, and they didn't mention my appearance, so I guessed that the part about immediate transformation applied to my inner self. Either that, or my hair looked so bad they chose to avoid the topic.

That night I slept very well. ("Not busy mind.")

The next morning I was astounded to find that the dark semicircles that had hung below my eyes for years were completely gone. Vanished! The delicate skin had not been harmed by vigorous herbal scrubbing; instead it was pale, white, glowing. I looked ten years younger.

The rest of my skin felt dramatically softer. Especially my legs, where the cowboys had scrubbed most vigorously—they were so silky-smooth I could hardly stop touching them. Also, my legs were now covered with tiny flakes of exfoliated-but-still-attached skin, perfect for the "doctor fish" downtown.

And I couldn't help wondering what would have happened if I had followed Wayan's instructions for other parts of my body—would they, too, have felt ten years younger? If so, what, exactly, would that entail? There was only one way to find out....

The Two Boys in Rural Argentina
Who Delighted in Showing Me Their Muscles

Yerba Maté

YACUYURÁ, ARGENTINA

Yerba maté must be the bitterest beverage ever brewed. I learned to drink it—and a great deal more—with an herbalist in the sweltering summer heat of an Argentine forest.

We met in a remote mountain village called Yacuyurá, a cluster of twenty or so small homes constructed of split logs and earth-colored plaster. A rutted dirt road was the only way into the settlement, which holds a place in time in the Sierras de Córdoba, that long saw-blade of peaks in north-central Argentina. Yacuyurá's residents raise poultry and hogs, coax corn and potatoes from the lean earth, and lug buckets of water up the hill from Arroyo las Lajas, a nearby stream that gurgles with sparkling water all year round.

The people of Yacuyurá work and cook and eat communally, participating in an ongoing, self-designed "experiment in human being" based on a harmonious relationship with the natural world. I had come to the Sierras de Córdoba to study a lifelong fascination—medicinal plants—and Yacuyurá provided our housing and other logistical support.

My teachers were Carlos, a handsome herbalist who had traveled more than four hundred miles from Buenos Aires to share his knowledge; and Amanda, a Colombian botanist who now teaches at the City University of New York. Carlos was lean and quick, like his city; Amanda was slow and heavy, like the forest itself. The two were attempting—successfully—to regain knowledge from grassroots sources, and then—somewhat less successfully—to reintroduce it to mainstream society.

Their mission is ambitious. Natural habitats are rapidly being destroyed here, as in many places, by profitable large-scale logging and ranching operations. Few herbalists remain, and very little local knowledge has been formally documented. Beginning in the 1950s, orthodox medicine taught that plant cures were dangerous because of their toxicity, and the old knowledge was suppressed. Here, as a consequence, it is all but lost, as traditional healers grow old and die before they are able to pass their knowledge on to a generation determined to leave their impoverished roots and move into the city—a generation enamored with the bright lights and take-an-asprin convenience of western culture.

We didn't know for sure whether our efforts would be of long-term value to the people who lived nearby or to the scientific community. Carlos and Amanda worked because they had a vision of people and plants living in harmony. They knew the plants; they had relationships with the plant spirits, and conversations with the bark and tendrils, the leaves and roots. For them, the work was a pleasure, like getting reacquainted with old friends at a high school reunion. For me the fieldwork was stultifying, the insects irritating. Overwhelming heat and humidity kept me sleepy during the day and restless at night, leaving me in a constant dream state. I continued only because Carlos and Amanda continued.

Amanda longed to understand the old ways. She wanted to explore the meaning of "health" in traditional cultures, as well as the environmental factors that contribute to the healing powers of plants. What does it mean to live without dis-ease? What parts of the plants are used to treat disease, and how are they prepared? What complementary components or procedures do the *curanderos* use? Amanda dreamed of moving medicinal plants from endangered logging areas to a small-but-safe preserve at Yacuyurá.

Carlos had studied plants all his life, and, as a young man, had apprenticed with a curandero—a traditional healer—near Yacuyurá. These mountains had been his home. But it's difficult to earn a living in the mountains, so Carlos moved to bustling Buenos Aires, where he now he owns a small herbal shop. More and more, his customers are foreign tourists.

We spent seven weeks together in the heavy, humid

forest, reaching back through history to rescue traditional knowledge, interviewing the few remaining local herbalists and documenting treatments, conducting demographic studies of the major medicinal species in order to learn their ecological requirements. Carlos identified plants, while Amanda and I roped off sectors of the forest with orange strings and calculated population density. We recorded daily high and low temperatures and rainfall, analyzed the soil, transplanted seedlings into a small nursery and mounted sample specimens in a big book.

Every morning, a stooped and wrinkled Yacuyurá elder led us through the forest, pointing out medicinal plants with her gnarled, shaky finger, and explaining their preparation and uses: Boil the bark; make a tea of leaves and stems; crush the young leaves for a poultice. In quiet moments, their names still loll on my tongue: *chañar*, used for treating coughs and bronchitis; *yerba meona*, a diuretic; *muerdago criollo* for parasites; *sombre del toro* for alcoholism. We gathered *jarilla, tala, abrojico, escobadura, quebracho blanco*, and many others. Some days we harvested *incayuyo*, a sacred herb used as a kidney and liver tonic. Other days we gathered bright red *mistol* berries to make cough syrup. Carlos and Amanda taught me to talk to the spirits of every plant. We always thanked them: "Thank you, jarilla spirit, for your contribution to our lives. Thank you, escobadura, for your wisdom and power. Thank you, incayuyo, for your selfless sacrifice today."

I would like to have tried some herbal cures myself, but I harbored no troubling parasites, did not suffer from a cough or bronchitis, and had no need of a poultice. My liver and kidneys seemed just fine. Besides, what if the doctors were right, and the herbs were dangerously toxic—could they cause irreparable damage? I asked Amanda, but she answered in a riddle: "Do not run." When I asked for clarification she advised, "Do not run toward them, or away."

On the day we made *arrope* (cough syrup), I decided to take a chance. The process was simple: In the morning, Carlos built a roaring wood fire, and suspended a huge black iron pot—a perfect witch's cauldron—over it. Water from the arroyo and a bushel of shiny red mistol berries bubbled for hours in the pot. Around noon, Amanda dumped in a ten-pound bag of white sugar—which seemed like cheating to me—and left the brew to simmer for the rest of the afternoon. Carlos kept adding wood to the fire, and Amanda occasionally stirred the pot with an oversized wooden spoon. That evening, after the mixture had cooled and thickened, I tested a spoonful. It tasted like cherries, and reminded me of the sickly-sweet Robitussin in my medicine cabinet back home. One sip was plenty.

The next evening Amanda whispered, "Carlos is a great herbalist, but his abilities in that arena are nothing compared with his mastery of the maté cere-mony. He will teach you to love the bitter herb, to go past the hard smokiness and into the heart of the maté."

Carlos was tall and broad-shouldered, with a high forehead, sparkling eyes, and a heavy black beard and mustache. His wavy hair was held back in a short, high ponytail with a baby blue elastic band. Although he mostly kept to himself, I had noticed Carlos drinking maté from a small gourd, which reminded me of a loyal dog—it seemed never to leave his side. Sometimes Carlos spat the stuff out onto the ground. I imagined it must taste terrible, and did not look forward to "being taught" to drink it. But Amanda insisted that the stuff was essential. "You will drink it," she com-manded, sitting me down at a weathered grey picnic table just as the sun was setting. "You will love it."

Carlos joined us; they had planned this. He set out a pot of hot water and a bag filled with the herb. "The drink is shared among family members or close friends, but never casually, nor in a restaurant," he explained. "Maté requires a ceremony."

The person who prepares the maté, usually the host, is called the *servidor*. The servidor fills the maté (a fist-sized hollow gourd) about two-thirds full with maté (yerba maté—the dried herb) and digs the *bombilla* (a stainless steel straw with a strainer at the bottom) down deep into the herb. Then he pours in hot water—slowly, very slowly. There's an art to this. The water must be very hot, but you don't want to have boiled the oxygen out of it, or the maté will taste flat. If tiny bubbles of bright green foam appear, you've done it right.

Out of courtesy, the servidor always drinks first, because the first bowlful is bitter. If it's too strong, the servidor spits out a mouthful.

After he has drunk it all, the servidor fills the gourd with hot water again, and passes the now-diluted brew to the next person ... who drinks it all and returns the maté (vessel) to the servidor, to be refilled for the next person. Everyone drinks from the same vessel and uses the same bombilla, and each person waits for a turn. Each time the maté is refilled, the drink becomes a little weaker.

If the maté is poured "short" (with too little water), a joking response is to say, "This is shorter than a pig's leg." If it's "long," one might respond with, "This is longer than the poor people's hope."

When I held onto the maté for a long time, talking rather than drinking, while the others patiently awaited their turns, Carlos teased me. "Give up the microphone," he said. "Are you trying to teach the maté to talk?"

He had seen through my ruse. I was afraid to taste the maté. But the time had come, and my friends were waiting. The maté gourd was round and warm and heavy in my hand—so comfortable. The bombilla, heated by the boiling water, had cooled enough that I could drink through it. Still, the metal was hot on my lips. I sucked the warm liquid into my mouth.

The taste of the maté was indescribable, but I will try: Imagine an extremely bitter, acrid, tea combined with partially-rotted vegetable matter. Now burn it slightly. That is the flavor of maté. Its aftertaste is milder, like roasted hay.

After I had swallowed several mouthfuls, I returned the gourd to Carlos. If he had noticed my discomfort, he ignored it. Each time I participated in a maté ceremony, I felt closer to my companions. And each time the gourd came around, the maté tasted a little better.

It is said that yerba maté seeds must pass through the digestive tract of a toucan before they can germinate. That is not strictly true, but perhaps it helps the tiny, temperamental seeds, which can take up to two years to sprout. The maté plant (*Ilex paraguayensis*) has very specific rainfall, humidity and temperature requirements. Attempts to grow it outside its native environment have consistently failed, but yerba maté is a major crop in South America, like tea or coffee in other parts of the world.

The Argentinian gauchos were supposedly so addicted to maté they would rather trade for it than for food. But the herb *is* a food, providing most of the phytonutrients necessary to sustain life, including significant amounts of several amino acids, vitamins, and minerals. Claiming the gauchos were addicted to it is like saying they were addicted to nutrition. Yerba maté is also said to "strengthen the nervous system"—whatever that means—and I admit that it put me in the mind of Argentina's famous magical realism on more than one occasion.

Every morning Amanda, Carlos, and I explored the forest around Yacuyurá, gathering plants and learning their properties from the old curandera. Every afternoon we shared maté in the shade of a spreading carob tree, enjoying the chocolate-scented pods overhead and the lazy buzz of nearby insects. In the haze of the drink and afternoon heat, even the flies seemed distant and benign. It took practice to get past the bitter, smoky flavor, but soon maté became a welcome respite from the sweltering afternoons, and an intimate ceremony of fellowship, nourishing my spirit as well as my body.

At the same time, the rainforest was opening up to me. The plant spirits were beginning to recognize my voice; the abrojico nodded when I passed. In some way the maté seemed to be mediating my understanding of the rainforest, teaching me a new way of communicating. How many other forest herbs held similar secrets? And how many would be lost forever after the loggers came through?

Early one morning, Amanda announced that we were going to skip our forest walk, and instead pay a visit to the barrio.

The barrio? I imagined poor people and garbage and

crime. *What on earth would I do in a barrio?*

"But I don't speak Spanish," I protested. "I can't be of any use in the barrio." Despite the fact that Amanda and I were from vastly different backgrounds, our friendship had grown deep as we worked side by side in the forest. I felt flattered that she had temporarily forgotten my language and botanical skills were not the same as hers. But I had no intention of putting myself in harm's way while she conducted whatever business she might have in the barrio. "I'll stay here today."

"You will come to the barrio," Amanda repeated. "You will be with the children."

Clearly, there was no use arguing. I attempted to determine what my tasks would be. Perhaps there was a school to be built or a well to be dug. I would not be very good at construction projects, but I could try. "What do you want me to do?"

"You will be with the children, just *be* with them."

"But what do you want me to *do*?"

Amanda didn't even try to explain. We loaded the commune's old white pickup truck with quebracho blanco seedlings and brought along a brown paper bag full of used pens and pencils someone had donated for the school.

Carlos drove us along narrow mountain roads to the barrio, a pleasant, if rickety, village. The residents were clean and dressed in American-style clothes. I didn't see any garbage or anyone who looked like a criminal. A cluster of boisterous children ran up to greet us, and Amanda and Carlos walked off to find the *curandera*, leaving me in a wide clearing with the children of the barrio.

Two little boys wearing nothing but matching brown shorts immediately began showing off, climbing a small tree and then pumping their arms to show me their muscles. I couldn't help laughing at their antics, and soon more children joined in, turning cartwheels, racing each other, vying for my attention. As the morning passed, we drew pictures of each other on a paper bag and played together with a balloon. Some of the children showed me what appeared to be a collection of sticks, which I examined appreciatively. I marveled at their joyful ease with the world around them, and found that I, too, had relaxed. This was surely the real meaning of health, the opposite of "dis-ease."

That afternoon we returned to Yacuyuá and sat, once again, beneath the carob tree. Carlos prepared the maté and we sipped it slowly, descending into the magic of the forest and its heat, the wafting scent of carob and the hazy buzz of insects.

And, at last, I understood Amanda's intent. Meeting the people who lived here, and getting to know them, was an essential part of learning about the forest. The plants and their properties, the people and their culture—all had evolved as a whole, and all were intertwined. The people of the barrio identified deeply with the land and its animals, soil, and plants. They were authentic ecologists—more so than the residents of Yacuyuá, who were working to live in harmony with the natural world. And more than the scientists who dreamed of unlocking the forest's secrets. I had traveled to Yacuyurá to study the ecology of medicinal plants, but what I came away with—what the maté ceremony and Amanda and Carlos and the children of the barrio had taught me—was a deeper understanding of human *being*.

Monument at the Cimetière du Père Lachaise

DEATH IN PARIS
PARIS, FRANCE

No matter where I went in Paris, Death was there, too. I shouldn't have been surprised, for Paris adores Death. She celebrates it, in fact. The City of Light's famous catacombs are a grand example, gleefully displaying a warning above their entrance: *Stop—This is the Empire of Death.* The remains of more than six million former Parisians rest sixty feet below, forming a never-ending labyrinth artfully lined with graceful femurs and cheek-to-cheek skulls, and open to tourists six days a week for the bargain price of eight Euros.

Three of Paris's major attractions are cemeteries: those in Montmartre and Montparnasse, and the celebrated Cimetière du Père Lachaise, where visitors pay daily tribute to Chopin and Balzac, Piaf and Wilde, Stein and Delacroix. Père-Lachaise feels right in early October, its trees letting loose wrinkled brown leaves, the sky like cold milk, the air still soft from summer.

I had my reasons for being at Père-Lachaise. My mother had died ten months earlier, after a tumultuous three-year relationship with cancer. My father died quite unexpectedly just four months after Mom, leaving me feeling achingly lonely for the first time in my life. The grief kept growing; it became a ravenous monster as I attended memorial services for an aunt and two friends in the space of four months. My uncle's health was failing, and a colleague was terminally ill. Friends and family dying—this was not part of my plan for my fifties. The adjustment was excruciating. I had a bone to pick with Death—a big one.

Yes, the Cimetière du Père Lachaise felt right. I walked there for hours, photographing headstones against the sky, kicking the husks of newly fallen prickly chestnuts, and inhaling the syrupy perfume of roses, gardenias and lilies—floral tributes to the recently deceased. I followed the crowds to Jim Morrison's grave and hunted in vain for Modigliani's.

Perhaps I had looked sad earlier in the week. A Parisian had remarked—out of nowhere—that visiting Père-Lachaise and touching Allan Kardec's gravestone would produce "good vibes." Heaven knows we need as many of those as we can get.

Kardec was a nineteenth-century Parisian educator and the founder of the Spiritualist Movement. Fresh flowers smothered his tombstone, which bore an inscription at the top: *Naître, mourir, renaître encore et progresser sans cesse, telle est la loi.* ("To be born, die, again be reborn, and so progress unceasingly, such is the law.") I shared twenty silent minutes there with a fleshy-faced, red-haired man wearing green pants, who apparently felt Kardec's vibes. I did not.

Wordless, we both departed.

Enough of chasing Death—I needed to move on.

But Paris would not allow it. In the Louvre I had hoped to enjoy masterpieces of Renaissance painting and sculpture, but found myself magnetically attracted to what looked like a shiny golden hand. It rose like a lighthouse in the middle of one room, its sparkling beacon winking in every direction. The wrist was cuffed with an elaborately decorated bracelet, the forearm clothed in silver encrusted with gilded coins, quartz crystals, and intricate cut-away red and blue enamel geometrics. The sign said it was a reliquary, manufactured in Naples between 1336 and 1338 for the hand of St. Luke. Was Death waving to me?

Reliquaries are containers for holy relics, important in Christian, Buddhist, Hindu and other religious traditions. Saints' body-part relics are significant because the spirit of the saint is said to live on—in some mysterious way—in the bodily remains. Reliquaries were also particularly important to French kings, who often specified (for reasons unfathomable to me) that their hearts be interred in a different location from their main burial places.

There was a whole room full of reliquaries. Death had followed me to the Louvre.

Thinking history and architecture might be a refreshing change of pace, I signed up for a tour with David

Downie, a Paris-based American journalist and novelist. David knows all the best places in the City of Light. He took me to St-Paul–St-Louis, a seventeenth-century baroque cathedral that, as it turned out, exalts the pickled heart of Louis XIV with a place of honor in a lustrous golden reliquary.

I caught a glimpse of it—the shining reliquary, not the heart itself—and later learned of an alternate theory about the final resting place of Louis XIV's heart: The Sun King's pickled organ may have been *eaten* by one Rev. Dr. William Buckland, an acclaimed Victorian theologian, geologist and paleontologist.

Like many of the great minister/naturalists of his time, the Rev. Buckland understood science and religion as complementary, rather than opposing, ways to view the world. He even believed that geological evidence demonstrated the truth of the great biblical flood.

Idiosyncratic as well as accomplished, Buckland pioneered the use of fossilized feces to scientifically analyze geohistory, and wrote the first full description of what would later be called a dinosaur. He was also a zoophagist whose lifelong ambition was to eat an example of every animal in existence.

Buckland was already well on his way to accomplishing that goal when he attended a dinner hosted by the Archbishop of York, at which the heart of Louis XIV—reportedly ensconced in a silver snuffbox owned by the Archbishop—was passed around the table for visitors to admire.

When it arrived at his plate, Buckland, an honored guest, announced, "I have eaten many strange things, but I have never eaten the heart of a king," and before anyone could stop him, the eccentric geologist is said to have swallowed the heart of Louis XIV. (If this account is true, I leave it to the reader's imagination to determine the heart's final resting place.)

Remembering my father, a scientist at heart, I escaped the church and headed to the Panthéon to see Foucault's pendulum. An exact copy of the pendulum swings from a 220-foot cable hung in the Panthéon's highest dome, demonstrating the rotation of the earth just as the original did in 1851. Physics and mechanics, arcs and curves, a brass ball gliding across the room minute after minute, hour after hour, day after day—these dry certainties calmed my spirit.

Death tracked me again, though, as I explored the Panthéon's lower chambers. Twenty feet below the pendulum lies a cavernous mausoleum. Its pale limestone walls—dry and powdery, like dust—and elegant vaulted ceilings shelter the remains of a hundred French luminaries, from Victor Hugo and Emile Zola to Marie Curie and Louis Braille. Even the ornate crypts of philosophers Voltaire and Rousseau each have a special spot beneath the Panthéon. The place was beautiful, but all those crypts gave me the shivers.

Death was everywhere. I gave in.

My next stop was the celebrated taxidermy shop that has stood on tony rue du Bac for more than one hundred fifty years. Deyrolle (*"Taxidermie, entomologie, curiosités naturelles"*) provides the world with majestically mounted tigers and bears, bright birds and butterflies, collections of curvaceous shells and boxes of pin-punctured beetles, all in the name of scientific inquiry. I have collected insects and done some taxidermy myself, and hoped that in Deyrolle I would find some sort of solace, a sense of the inevitability of death intertwined with an appreciation of the majesty of nature.

Two stuffed gazelles, standing on their hind legs and dressed as humans, greeted me in the first floor entryway. One wore a plain white button-down shirt, the other a bright red gardening apron. Each held out an engraved silver serving tray, as though they were butlers at a fancy party. Death and whimsy—a promising start.

But I was unprepared for the shock of what I saw up-stairs. A large, hardcover book was on prominent display. The elegant volume, *1000 Degrees Centigrade: Deyrolle*, documents a four-alarm fire that burned so hot—1000 degrees centigrade—that it decimated Deyrolle's *Wunderkammer* (wonder-rooms) in the winter of 2008. The photographer's surreal subjects, from eviscerated goats to roasted butterflies, are twisted and disfigured, melted and crusted.

Shaken, I could not leave Deyrolle, and wandered for hours amongst its taxidermied menagerie—the frozen zebra family, three huge and inexplicably sad-looking flop-eared white rabbits, a fuzzy infant yak that looked like it was about to take its first step, a benign glass-eyed grizzly—returning again and again to the mesmerizing book with its deformed and fragile images.

I was only released from Deyrolle's spell after a visit to the butterfly room, where dozens of breathtaking beauties spiraled their way from floor to ceiling, and hundreds more floated in eternal, orderly rows behind glass. I asked a shopkeeper whether visitors ever complained about all the dead animals at Deyrolle. "They cannot." She shrugged with Parisian nonchalance. "We are one hundred percent legal."

One hundred percent legal—just like death itself. Just as Allan Kardec had said: "To be born, die, again be reborn, and so progress unceasingly, such is the law."

There was one more place I needed to visit in Paris. My college days are a distant memory, but as a philosophy major, I wanted to pay my respects at the grave of René Descartes, the groundbreaking "Father of Modern Philosophy" who left generations of thinkers pondering the maxim: *I think, therefore I am.* His difficult-to-dispute assertion raised far more questions than it answered, and had driven me to distraction for years.

Given the importance of final resting places in

France, I expected a grand reliquary for Descartes. His tomb is in Paris's oldest church, the Eglise de Saint-Germain-des-Prés, erected in the sixth century and a center of intellectual life in the French Catholic church until the Revolution, twelve hundred years later. Its gothic rib-vaulted ceilings soar, slate blue, punctuated with gold-leaf stars that twinkle in the incense-filled light far above the altar. If you listen well, you can hear the echoes of intonations from centuries past.

The tombstone was unremarkable. It was barely even visible in its small, dark chapel on the south side of the church. I moved forward until a velvet rope pushed against my legs. The towering nave stood on my right, its dust motes dancing in the ruby light that filtered through a stained-glass window. To my left, gilded arches supported mythological figures frozen in a silent, byzantine conversation. They may have been discussing the nature of the human mind, or the essence of material things—a twelve-hundred-year conversation.

"Nice job sideswiping Aristotle," I whispered into the darkness.

"Someone had to do it," Descartes replied, in a voice that was not as strong as I would have expected. It had to be Descartes. I peered into the shadows and no one else was there. "You know about my dreams, don't you?" he continued.

One night when he was twenty-three, Descartes

famously had a series of dreams that he interpreted to mean he should set out to reform all of the world's knowledge—including Aristotelian physics—and develop a comprehensive theory explaining everything.

"Yes, the whole mind-body problem, what we now call *Cartesian dualism*," I began. I had been obsessed with the mind-body problem since I was a teenager. It is intimately linked to other important issues, including the questions of free will—which my mother believed to be the most significant conundrum of all time—and the possibility of immortality, a subject my recent obsession with death had been skirting. "There must have been another way—after all, dualism introduces so many problems."

"There was no other way," Descartes insisted. "I had to begin at the beginning, with the one indisputable fact: *I think*. From there, it was just a short and com- pletely logical step to *I think, therefore I am*. I directly experience thinking, and there must be an entity *doing* the thinking, and that entity is, by definition, me. It's quite elegant." And with that, the Father of Modern Philosophy slipped into the darkness.

A little bit of my pain disappeared along with him. Paris had shown me how to celebrate death, how to embrace it with reliquaries and taxidermy and cata-combs. And Descartes had shown me that in the end, all we can do with a great mystery is allow it to disappear into the darkness.

*Driveway at the Entrance to the All Seasons Glen Helen
Homestead, which has Since been Renamed
the Glen Helen Resort*

Keys to the Outback
Glen Helen, Australia

"I can't believe you left them there," Jim muttered as I squeezed the handle and pulled hard for a third time.

"What do you mean, you can't believe it? You can see them as well as I can. You're not going blind, are you?" The keys were clearly visible in the ignition. People were beginning to stare.

He walked around to my side of the car. "I *knew* this would happen if I let you drive."

"It has nothing to do with my driving." I circled to the passenger side to try that handle again. "My driving was *fine*. It's not as though *you've* never locked keys in the car." I wasn't entirely certain he ever had, but was willing to gamble on it to make my point. I wanted desperately to defend myself, because I suspected my mistake would have serious consequences.

We had rented our Holden wagon in Darwin, 300 miles away. At first, the man at the A1 Car Rental company tried to give us an old beater: no radio, one broken window, lots of dents, the whole thing covered in powdery red dust. "Yir goin' tuh Katherine? This's yir car, mate!"

175

The salesman looked at us incredulously when we complained. After some verbal wrangling, my husband, who is large and can be quite persuasive, managed to get us a late model station wagon with intact windows and a weak-but-functioning air conditioner.

Knowing we were in for long expanses of empty highway, we stopped at the edge of town to top off the fuel tank. "What's the speed limit, anyway?" Jim asked the gas station attendant.

"What kin ya do, mate?"

"I said, 'What's the speed limit on the highway to Katherine?'" Jim repeated himself cheerfully. He meets strangers easily.

"What kin ya do?"

We hadn't anticipated any troubles communicating with the locals on our trip Down Under, but that had been naïve. Their accents were difficult to understand, the rhyming slang was impossible to decipher, and the wry Aussie sense of humor kept me off balance. I had become resigned to the fact that I was clueless much of the time, but Jim liked to maintain a sense of control.

About an hour out of Darwin we stopped to take each other's picture standing next to what the Aussies call "anthills." These aren't mere bumps of soft dirt, like American anthills. They are towering structures, sometimes as much as twenty feet high, built by termites out of their own saliva and feces. The resulting substance is so hard that the anthills were ground up and used instead of concrete to make airplane runways during World War II. Or so the Aussies said, and I believed them.

The instant we climbed out of the car, flies covered us both. Flies! Making themselves at home on my bare arms, crawling up my legs, doing their best to creep into my eyes and mouth. I tried desperately to shoo them away, but the flies were not deterred; they crawled over us with impunity. Billions of them live there—maybe trillions. I read that there are more than 650 separate species in Australia. The air was hot—easily 105°F—and the land stretched out flat and dusty, with sparse vegetation and even fewer animals. I couldn't imagine how such a lifeless expanse could possibly support those buzzing hordes. What did they eat, anyway, when there were no tourists around?

We snapped our anthill photos fast and hopped back into the car. Hundreds of flies came with us. After some frantic experimentation, involving swatting, speeding, swerving, and swearing, we discovered that the best way to get rid of flies was to open all the windows and drive slowly. Of course this rendered the air conditioner useless, and we were soon dripping with perspiration, which caused the red Outback dust to cake onto our bodies in a most unattractive way. When I had exterminated all the flies but three, I climbed into the back seat and smashed the last survivors with our A1 rental papers. They left dry, brown smears across the part where we had declined extra insurance. Then we rolled up the windows and drove in silence, waiting for the car to cool off. It was too hot to talk.

As it turned out, there was, indeed, no official speed limit on the road to Katherine. Hundreds of miles of open road, dead straight, no highway patrol. The speed limit was whatever you could coax your car to do. I say "coax" because only a fool would take a high performance car on this road. When we stopped to get the camera, I discovered that the inside of the trunk was covered with fine red dust. The dust was also sucked into our luggage, and, inside that, into the plastic bag I use to protect the camera from dust. It gets into the engine, too, and the brakes. That was why the rental company had at first provided us with a beater for the trip. I began to feel guilty that we were ruining this A1 car for anything but Outback travel.

There were "speed limit" signs on the road: white rectangles with a big black zero in the center, and a slanted bar crossing the zero. ("What kin ya do?") Jim took full advantage of this once-in-a-lifetime opportunity, and opened it up on the open road. When the speedometer hit 130 kilometers, I looked away. Mostly the trip was OK, and even seemed fairly safe, because there were no other vehicles on the road. A couple of times we hit potholes and bounced hard. Once there was a really loud noise, and when I looked in the mirror I thought I saw something fall off the bottom of the car. But it was getting late, and we kept driving until we got to Katherine.

The next morning, the car seemed fine, and we took a dirt road out to Glen Helen, which is an outpost in the middle of nowhere. It consists of one gasoline pump, two camels in a small corral, a permanent-looking "No Vacancy" sign, and a small motel-and-bar combination called the All Seasons Glen Helen Homestead.

There isn't much to do in Glen Helen, except to take a hike up the gorge, which is a dramatic contrast to the rest of the Outback. It was fun at first: A small stream gurgled along the trail, there were a few hardy plants, and the steep canyon walls sheltered us from the sun. Here and there a small gray lizard skittered out of our path, but other than that, it was dead quiet. After a while we were too hot even in the shade, and we were tired and hungry, so we walked back to the roadhouse.

This is when we discovered I had locked the keys in the car. We had left our wallets safely in the glove compartment, since we wouldn't need them on the hike. (No need to carry any more than was necessary.) When we returned, we needed money to buy a couple of cold beers and some tucker (food). So there we were, circling the car, tugging the handles, arguing, hot and tired and hungry.

My clothes were sticking to my body. A fly landed on Jim's face, and walked into his nose. Until you have witnessed it, you cannot imagine how intensely irritable it makes a person when a fly crawls into his nostril and refuses to be dislodged.

It was at this point that we had the conversation about my driving.

Several helpful folks wandered over to view the keys dangling from the ignition and offer advice. "Why donja jis use yir spair key, mate?" one asked.

"This woonda happened if you'da left yir windars open," another offered.

The most practical of the lot suggested we simply throw a brick through the window, "She'll be right, mate!" When you're in the Outback, life seems fairly straightforward.

But there were no bricks to be had in Glen Helen, so I went inside, bummed some change, and phoned A1. It turned out the only spare key was in their Alice Springs office, more than 800 miles away. They said they'd send someone right over, as soon as they could round up an airplane. "No worries."

Waiting for the car keys to be delivered, Jim chatted up the waitress at the All Seasons Glen Helen Homestead—as I recall, he was not speaking to me at that time—and expressed his disgust over the hundreds of flies crawling on the outside of the window.

"Awwr that's nothin', mate!" she responded. "In the summa they completely cuvah ervery winda, so no light comes in uh'tall. Keeps the place coolah that way."

Hours passed. It was late afternoon, and I began to worry about where we would spend the night. There were no vacant rooms at the Homestead, and I was sure the Outback was at least as inhospitable at night as it was during the day. We couldn't even sleep in the car. There was no one to hitch a ride back to Katherine with; the travelers who were not staying the night had long since left. It was beginning to look like Jim might spend the night with the waitress, but what about me? I tried to remember whether Bedouins or other desert people slept with their camels, but could only dredge up stories of mean-spirited animals that spit and kicked at humans.

I was in the middle of wondering whether lizards, which of course are cold-blooded, would be attracted to my body heat if I were sleeping in the desert, when a cheerful man in short shorts and an A1 shirt appeared and handed Jim the key, no worries. What did we owe him for this extravagant kindness? "Awwr, nothin' mate." He gave Jim a friendly slap on the back. "We'll sen'ja the bill laytah."

They did, too. Five months later a charge for $65 showed up on my credit card bill. Sixty-five dollars— not even enough to pay for the airplane fuel! The description said simply, "A1 key delivery." Life *is* fairly straightforward in the Outback.

The Namorona River in Madagascar,
Which I would Love to Visit Again

Speaking Malagasy
RANOMAFANA, MADAGASCAR

Other people's children cause your nostrils to flare.
This is my favorite, so far, of Madagascar's thousands
of witty proverbs. The culture is rich with song and
dance, poetry and proverb and metaphor. Eloquence
is such an important part of life, in fact, that according
to Madagascar's classic collection of folklore, "It is the
master of the words who rules the kingdom."

But if the kingdom is rich in eloquence, her people—
the Malagasy—are impoverished. Many struggle every
day for immediate needs like food, water, and medical
care. In spite of this, the people are hopeful and
resilient. They love the "Land of our Ancestors", so
much that if a Malagasy leaves the island, he takes
along a pocketful of soil to ensure a safe return. It was
in this poor and hopeful land that I received the gift of
a lifetime.

I was in Madagascar doing volunteer field research,
helping scientists who study the endangered lemurs
that live on the island. I arrived in the crowded capital
city of Antananarivo, where I learned to say *tsy misy*,
"there isn't any," to the flocks of children begging in

the streets, pushing their way to our minibus, pressing eagerly against my body when I walked in the city center. The city children asked for money or for a *bonbon*, and even after it was clear I had neither to offer, they wanted to touch me, touch my clothing. They smiled and chattered and studied my white skin and light hair.

Ranomafana, the nearest town to our research center, is more rural than Antananarivo. The children here usually ask for a *stilo* (pen), although they rarely attend school and are too poor to have access to paper. There's no economic advantage in attending school, which steals away productive hours for working in the fields. With high mortality rates, large families, and short life expectancies—the average is fifty-five years— immediate needs are people's most pressing concerns. School has no connection to subsistence; it is simply a place children might go to socialize with friends for a few hours if it's a slow day in the rice paddies.

The other researchers all spoke English, so there was technically no need for me to learn the local language. Which was a good thing, because I found even a simple sentence—such as *Excuse me, where is the market? (Aiza no misy ny tsena, aza fady?)*—incomprehensible. *It is still difficult for me to understand what people say* translates to *Mbola sarota amiko ny mahazo izay lazain'ny olona.* I was conversationally challenged, to say the least.

One bright Saturday morning I walked from camp

into town with Elaine, a spirited social worker from southern California who was volunteering with me. Along the way we met a local girl. She was as tattered a child as I've ever seen, wrapped—even in the tropical heat—in ragged layers I couldn't identify as articles of clothing. Her bare feet were covered in dust and seemed to grow out of the ground as she stood, frozen, eying us from the edge of the road where a patch of the island's jungle rose up.

The girl couldn't have been more than five or six years old, yet she was completely alone. Her arms were full of green-leafed branches, which she was carrying down the hill, probably into Ranomafana town for her mother to sell at the market. The girl still had more than a mile to go, and, as that was our destination as well, Elaine and I looked forward to sharing the walk with her.

"*Salama*. Hello." I stood in the middle of the wide dirt road, smiling hopefully at the little girl and calling out the only word I could remember.

No response. I regretted that I had not bothered to learn the language. Elaine and I said our names and pointed to ourselves, then pointed to the girl, asking her name. Perhaps the child would understand our pantomime and inflection, if not our words. The girl studied us, then slowly extended the armful of wild herbs she was carrying, even though we stood more than thirty feet away. She began to follow us, keeping her distance, yet obviously eager to interact. Her dark eyes sparkled with anticipation.

Madagascar is like that child. It is a young country, melodic, hopeful, and poor. It is so remote as to be almost wild. And it is slipping into the sea. Torrential tropical rains—the same rains that have given life to the forests for millions of years—now wash barren dirt down the mountain slopes, drive nutrients through gullies, into rivers, out to sea. Viewed from the air, Madagascar's red earth bleeds from its rivers into the Indian Ocean. Without vegetation to provide transpiration, cloud formation is slowed, and rainfall decreases. Over time, rainforests morph into deserts, food becomes scarce, and indigenous species die out. There is not much left.

The Malagasy have traditionally subsisted with slash-and-burn farming: cultivating a piece of land for a few seasons until the soil's fertility is exhausted, then moving on and allowing the soil to regenerate. This agricultural strategy works very well as long as there is enough area to support it. But the people in Madagascar have run out of land, and the land has run out of time.

There didn't seem to be much left in our interaction with the little girl, either. We did not speak Malagasy. Our pantomime had failed. Five minutes into our interaction, salama no longer seemed appropriate. I was visiting a country that held eloquence in the highest regard, yet I was mute.

Fortunately, Elaine was clever. She whistled a short sequence—the first three notes from the *Close Encounters of the Third Kind* theme song—and the little girl whistled back. Elaine responded with a longer sequence, all five notes, and the girl puckered up and whistled back in perfect pitch. Then the child whistled her own melody to us, and, as we whistled in reply, she approached, extending her thin arms and thrusting the herbs toward us.

I reached out and rubbed a small leaf between my thumb and forefinger, then sniffed it, hoping both to communicate and to identify the herb. But the scent, like the language, was foreign. I could only shrug and smile appreciatively.

That was enough. The girl became our wary companion, skipping alongside Elaine and me, always at arm's length, whistling her tunes and ours, and finally singing us a lovely song in her small, faraway voice. When we reached the bustling marketplace in Ranomafana town she slipped into the sea of faces, leaving Elaine and me to wander, scanning the crowd for her shy smile, straining to hear a song or a whistle. We searched for more than an hour but never saw her again. Eventually we trudged back to camp, feeling sad and oddly empty. We hadn't even learned her name.

Even so, that child left me with the greatest gift I have ever received—gratitude. As I thought about her life, I appreciated my good fortune to have been born into an affluent time and place, where I can take things like running water, electricity, and relative economic stability pretty much for granted. Gratitude for food and shelter, heat and clothing, for my good health and education, for books and cats and cozy carpeting, safety pins and Gore-Tex and ponytail scrunchies ... I could go on and on—and that's the point.

Back at camp, I picked up a handful of dirt to bring home. Rather than causing my nostrils to flare, the Malagasy children had charmed me. I wanted to return to Madagascar, to hear their melodic voices, to be inspired by these people who knew how to live eloquent lives despite their simple lifestyle.

Sometimes I find myself feeling angry at circumstances beyond my control, deprived of something I want badly, or indignant about some perceived unfairness. On those occasions, I need only whistle the first five notes of *Close Encounters* in order to remember how much I have to be thankful for. The little Malagasy girl had spoken to me in a profound way—without ever saying a word.

Crossroads in the Middle of Nowhere

At a Crossroads

SOMEWHERE IN TUNISIA

I didn't know whether I was being kidnapped or rescued—that was what made my one big decision so difficult. That and the fact that I was young and foolish, and more than a little anxious about being stranded in the North African desert.

It all began quite innocently, as this sort of situation often does. Our bus had deposited Alan, my affable traveling companion, and myself at the door of a small, clean hotel in a dusty Tunisian village. The buildings were two stories high at most, covered with plaster, and white-washed against the powdery red dust that enveloped the town and seemed to stretch forever. In the desperate heat of late afternoon, the place appeared to be completely deserted. Not a single shop was open and the dirt streets were empty: no vehicles, no pedestrians, not even a stray dog.

Inside, the 1940s-era hotel was as empty as the street. There were no brochures advertising nearby attractions (I suspected there *were* no nearby attractions); there was no "We accept VISA, MasterCard, and American Express" sign. That was okay; I had travelers' checks. There was no bouquet of silk flowers, no table, no couch on which weary travelers could rest. A lone white straight-backed chair stood sentry on the floor of exquisitely patterned blue and red ceramic tiles. The reception desk held a silver tray filled with mints.

I had only just met Alan, a wandering college student like myself, that morning. But I quickly decided he'd be great to travel with: He seemed friendly, calm and reasonable—not the type to freak out if a bus schedule changed or a train was delayed. Plus he spoke a little French, which I did not. Alan had a quick, cryptic conversation with the hotel clerk, and then translated for me. The clerk had suggested that he hitch a ride to the local bar/restaurant—six miles out of town—for a beer and a bite to eat. It didn't occur to either of us that a woman shouldn't also venture out, and I was eager to see some sights, meet the locals, and have dinner. Of course I went along.

In retrospect, I realize I should have known better. We were in Tunisia, a country where women stay indoors and cover up like caterpillars in cocoons. The guidebooks had warned me to cover my shoulders and legs, and I felt quite modest and accommodating in a loose button-up shirt and baggy jeans.

When we arrived, I found that the place was more bar than restaurant, and that I was the only female present. Even the waiters were all men. But these details didn't seem important. After all, I had dressed conservatively, and decided to take the precaution—

again, recommended by my guidebook—of avoiding direct eye contact with men. What could possibly go wrong?

Since I spoke neither French nor Arabic—and was assiduously avoiding eye contact—it was quite impossible for me to converse with anyone but Alan, who was busy putting his first-year college language skills to dubious use. I was bored. This was a plain-as-bread sort of establishment; there was no big screen TV soccer game, no video arcade, not even a friendly game of cards for me to watch. Just a lot of dark men in white robes, sitting in mismatched wooden chairs, speaking softly in a language I could not understand and drinking tiny cups of strong coffee. The bitter, familiar aroma was a meager comfort.

Then the music began; it sounded off-key and was startlingly loud and foreign—a little frightening, even. Next the belly dancers appeared: twelve gorgeous women, one after another, with long, dark hair, burnished skin, flowing diaphanous skirts in brilliant vermilion and aqua and emerald, gold necklaces, belts, bracelets, anklets. Gold everywhere: tangled cords jangling against long brown necks; fine, weightless strands decorating the swirling fabrics; heavy gold chains slapping in a satisfying way against ample abdominal flesh. They were a remarkable contrast to the stark room and simple furnishings, and I began to realize that things in Tunisia were not entirely as they first appeared.

193

The music quickened, and the dancers floated across the bar—which had somehow been converted into a stage—and around the room, weaving in and out among tables, lingering occasionally for a long glance at a pleased patron. Soon they were at our table, looking not at Alan but at me, urging me, with their universal body language, to join them.

Did I dare? My stomach clenched momentarily. I knew my dancing would be clumsy and ugly next to theirs, my short-cropped hair and lack of makeup unattractively boyish, my clothing shapeless and without style or significant color. I wore no jewelry—as the guidebook suggested—just my glasses, which were not particularly flattering.

Of course I was relatively unattractive and clumsy in this foreign environment, I thought, but there was no need to be priggish as well. And the women were by now insistent, actually taking me by both hands and pulling me up to dance with them. Flushed with embarrassment, I did my best to follow their swaying hips and graceful arm movements as we made our way around the room once again. Even with the aid of the two beers, I was not foolish enough to attempt to duplicate their astonishing abdominal undulations.

As soon as I thought these exotic, insistent beauties would allow it, I broke the line and resumed my place—plain, awkward, very white, and completely out of my element—next to Alan. Thereafter, it was excruciatingly embarrassing for me to watch the dancers, and Alan agreed to accompany me back to the hotel. He, too, had had enough excitement for the evening and was ready to retire, so he asked the bartender to call us a cab. A fellow bar patron overheard the conversation and was kind enough to offer us a lift. The man wore Western-style clothing, understood Alan's French, and seemed safe enough; we felt fortunate to have arranged the ride in spite of our limited linguistic abilities and the fact that the night was still young.

But that's when the evening turned ugly.

Two well-dressed, middle-aged men left the bar immediately after we did. We saw them get into a black Mercedes, and we watched in the rear-view mirror as they trailed us, just our car and theirs, bumping along a sandy road in the empty desert. There were no buildings, streetlights or pedestrians, and we saw no other vehicles.

I looked out the window, enjoying the vast, black night sky and trying to ignore my growing sense of anxiety. When we came to an unmarked Y intersection, our driver, in a bizarrely ineffective attempt at deception, headed steadily towards the road on the right, then veered off at the last second to take the road on the left. Neither Alan nor I could remember which direction we'd come from hours earlier, when it was still light out and we were not under the spell of Tunisian music and belly dancers and beer. The strange feigning and last-second careening alarmed us both.

And it got worse.

Immediately after the incident at the intersection, the men in the car behind us revved the engine, chased us down and ran us off the road and into a ditch. They stood in the road, shouting and gesticulating wildly outside our car. My hands went icy in the warm night air. Despite—or perhaps because of—an imposing language barrier, we had the impression that the men who ran our car off the road were attempting to rescue us.

But what, exactly, were they rescuing us from? Was our driver a sociopathic kidnapper bent on selling us into slavery? A rapist? A murderer? And why were our "rescuers" so insistent? Was it out of the goodness of their hearts, or did they, too, have some sinister motive? We had to make a choice. One car would probably take us safely to our hotel; the other might lead to a terrifying fate. But we had no idea which was which.

In this moment of crisis, we clenched hands and Alan looked at me—somewhat desperately, I thought—for a decision. I tried to assess his strength, and wondered whether he was a good fighter. (Probably not—he was a Yale man.) My stomach churned, but I forced myself to concentrate. We had only two options: We could remain in the long black limo, hope it could be extricated from the ditch, and hope our volunteer driver really was the kind and innocuous man he had appeared to be.

Or we could bolt from the car, scramble out of the ditch, and as quickly as possible, put our rescuers and their car between ourselves and the man who had so generously offered us a ride. The two men were still shouting, and began to pound and slap the driver's window. Even so, Alan leaned towards staying. After all, he reasoned, it was only one man, and there were two of us. Surely we could overpower him and escape if it proved necessary.

I wanted to bolt. Even though there were two men in the "rescue" car, as opposed to only one in our vehicle, I had become certain, in some wholly subjective way, that our man was crazy, and I'd heard that crazy people can be quite strong. Plus, our apparent rescuers, the men who had just run us off the road, warned Alan that we were with "*un homme méchant! Mauvais!*"— A wicked man. But the deciding factor was that these two men had actually gone to the trouble of following us out of the bar, chasing us down, running our car off the road and into a dusty ditch, and were now expending a great deal of energy trying to convince us of something.

Surely that constellation of actions bespoke a serious purpose, such as rescuing two foolish young travelers from a lifetime of misery in the North African desert. The two men *must* be rescuers; kidnappers were not likely to go to so much trouble, or to risk scratching or even denting their shiny black late-model Mercedes in the process.

Alan was no help; I had to make a decision myself, and quickly. But what about the downside? In the middle of all the commotion—and with Alan sitting next to me looking more than a little uncertain—I realized that we had not yet fully considered the potential negative consequences of an incorrect choice. If we chose to stay, and it was the wrong choice, the man would undoubtedly drive us to some sort of central kidnapping headquarters—probably an impenetrable, fortress-like stone building with dark, echoing corridors, or perhaps a sweltering, waterless hovel cleverly hidden in remote, sand-swept dunes. In that case, he would have a knife, or a gun, or evil partners—or perhaps all of the above—and the fact that the two of us probably could have overpowered him would be moot. We would be goners.

On the other hand, if we bolted, and *that* was the wrong choice, we would be double-goners because the two men could also turn out to be kidnappers or murderers who could easily overpower us. Downsides being equally awful, we decided to go with our gut. Or guts. The problem was that Alan's gut said *stay*, and mine said *bolt*.

Fortunately, it didn't occur to either of us to split up. Eventually I was able to convince Alan to bolt, which we did with great vigor, clawing through weeds and rocks and sand, out of the ditch, onto the road, and into the cool, black car waiting in the darkness.

But even then we couldn't relax. As we rode off into the night—this time with *two* men in the front seat—

my stomach was still churning; we had no way of knowing whether we had made the right decision. What if these men were also evil? Perhaps we had been unwittingly trapped in some web of rival-kidnapping-gang intrigue from which there was no hope of escape. Or perhaps it had begun even earlier, with Alan's fractured French, or with my being the thirteenth dancer—and in pants.

Eventually our two rescuers returned us to the Y intersection, turned onto the right—and correct—road, and delivered us to the hotel without further incident. God forgive us, I'm pretty sure Alan and I were both too dazed to thank them. Well, we thanked them for the ride, but not for saving our lives.

Inside the hotel, my stomach calmed down, and my hands returned to their normal temperature. The stress began to drain from my body; at last I could enjoy the luxury of relief! Alan and I stood at the reception desk, looking into each others' eyes. He picked up a mint from the silver bowl and ate it. I could smell it on his breath. The entrance hall was cool and quiet; no one else was around.

"Well, that was quite an evening," he finally said.
"Yes, quite an evening," I agreed.
"Well, goodnight, then."
"OK, goodnight."
I walked upstairs, puked, and went to bed.

Folkdancers in Dubrovnik, Wearing Embroidered Costumes that Could Very Well Have Been Made by Women from Desa.

Silk from Ashes

DUBROVNIK, CROATIA

"We let them wear our underwear," Jan Hasnal recounts. "Refugees streamed in from the countryside. We started where we could, sharing whatever we had in our homes. The women made queues, waiting for soup or powdered milk. They had nothing; they couldn't even cook their own meals."

Hasnal is explaining what life has been like in Dubrovnik since the devastating Homeland War of 1991 to 1995, when Croatia declared independence from Yugoslavia. She tells me her story—the story of 11,640 tiny eggs, her bra, and heroic transmutation.

Dubrovnik, "The Pearl of the Adriatic," is a labyrinth of white stone buildings, red rooftops, and green shuttered windows. To the north and east stretch forests of oak and pine; to the south and west, sandy beaches and transparent turquoise waters. The soil is thin and rocky, yielding little, but residents have scraped out a living for centuries.

This is a city that once rivaled Venice with its prowess in shipping, trade and diplomacy, though you wouldn't guess it from the smallish harbor in the medieval Old Town. And according to some historians, Dubrovnik had the highest Gross Domestic Product in the world during her golden age from the fourteenth to sixteenth centuries. But these successes, along with her strategic position on the Silk Road, left the city-state ripe for plunder, and Dubrovnik was besieged by invaders over and over again.

Ruled successively by the Byzantine, Venetian, Hungarian, and Turkish empires, this wealthy merchant republic encircled itself with protective turrets and towers; in some places the city's fortified walls are as much as twenty feet thick. But that was not enough to stop Napoleon's forces as they lobbed 3,000 cannon-balls at Dubrovnik in 1806. Italians and Germans occupied the city during World War II. And in the freezing December of 1991, Serbian forces attacked and laid siege, ruthlessly cutting off all water and electricity, reducing centuries-old buildings to rubble, and blanketing the pale city with smoke and ash. Dubrovnik was devastated, but her citizens endured.

I am on the Dalmatian Coast as part of a World Leaders Symposium, visiting places like Croatia, Bosnia and Herzogovina, Serbia, and Montenegro, and seeing for myself the places where recent history was made. The trip is especially meaningful because my travel companions include world leaders who helped *make* that history: Dr. Madeleine Albright, for one, who served as the U.S. Ambassador to the United Nations from 1993 to 1997, and as U.S. Secretary of State from 1997 to 2001, and whose controversial decisions ultimately helped NATO bring an uneasy peace to the Balkans. Peter Galbraith, U.S. Ambassador to the Republic of Croatia from 1993 to 1998 and a principal architect of the 1995 Erdut Agreement that ended the war in Croatia, is here, as is William Perry, U.S. Secretary of Defense from 1994 to 1997.

We explore ancient walled cities like Dubrovnik with its modern shrapnel scars; Sarajevo, with its Islam, Jewish, Catholic, Orthodox, and Evangelical places of worship; and Mostar with its sinuously hump-backed Stari Bridge, a symbol of historic friendships and current reunification efforts. We hear our lecturers' perspectives on what worked and what didn't work in Bosnia and Croatia, as well as local politicians' hopeful visions of a multi-ethnic future for the region. And we hear chilling war stories like Jan Hasnal's.

Hasnal was in Dubrovnik in the 1990s, helping with the relief efforts. "When war has happened to you, that is different from seeing it on the television in your living room. Thousands were displaced. Old ladies—they arrived carrying plastic bags with all their things. They were cousins of the people I bought fruit from at the market; they were the mothers of my friends. I saw fear and disaster in their eyes.

"We put the refugees in hotels. The Red Cross sent clothes," she remembers, "but you had to sign an affidavit if you received even one shirt—it was humiliating. We needed to find some work for the refugees, so we cut up good clothes into strips and the women put them back together into recycled garments, to keep their fingers busy, to help their mental health.

"One old lady asked me, 'My dear, can you bring me a silkworm? I am very ashamed to be wearing my neighbor's clothing.' I asked the authorities, but they were no help. They thought because of the bombing someone in Dubrovnik had gone crazy, asking for silkworms instead of food."

Why silkworms? Dubrovnik and silkworms go back a long way. The Chinese, who discovered silk, guarded it zealously. But according to legend, two monks smuggled silkworm eggs and mulberry seeds out of China inside hollow bamboo canes, letting the rest of the world in on the secret. For hundreds of years, silk was traded along with other precious commodities— gold and silver, pepper and spices—and by the fifteenth century Dubrovnik supplied the elegant fabric to much of Europe. Rural Croatian women used a traditional method of raising silkworms, in which they wrapped the tiny silkworm eggs in cloth and placed them between their breasts, where it was warm and the eggs would hatch.

Perhaps this history of silken intrigue inspired Jan Hasnal. In 1993, she founded an organization called Desa, with the goal of helping both local women and the influx of refugees cope with the social and psychological horrors of war. Desa sponsored embroidery workshops in the refugee camps, providing a sense of purpose and the beginnings of economic independence for the women there.

Hasnal wanted to find silkworms so the women could reclaim their livelihoods, but was thwarted by a ban on transporting insects. She persevered for years, finally locating silkworm eggs in Lyon, France, and convincing women there to donate eleven grams of them—about two teaspoons full. A silkworm egg is the size of a pinpoint, and eleven grams are enough to produce 11,640 silkworms. Jan carried the tiny eggs the same way Croatian women had traditionally carried them—in her bra. "I couldn't get them across the border any other way," she explained. "Maybe it is the destiny of the silkworm to travel incognito."

Now, in a wooded valley near Dubrovnik, women once again produce silk thread the traditional way, beginning by carefully incubating the eggs of a blind, flightless moth, *Bombyx mori*. They feed fresh mulberry leaves to the young silkworms many times a day for more than a month. When the silkworms are fully grown—about three inches long—the creatures stop eating and begin to spin their fluffy white cocoons, which are ready to be harvested after four or five days. The cocoons are stirred in hot water and their delicate threads, sometimes as much as a kilometer in length, are reeled onto a holder, dried, and processed with soap and—ironically—with the ashes that once covered Dubrovnik.

The women of Desa use silk thread and their embroidery skills to recreate the area's traditional folkloric costumes, replacing heirlooms that were destroyed during the war. Intricate red and gold embroidery, tassels and cross-stitches, floral and geometric patterns, brightly colored scarves and sashes and blouses and jackets—all have reappeared in Dubrovnik.

These women endured bombs and occupation, siege and starvation ... and they found a way to transmute ashes and silkworms into dignity and independence. All with the help of 11,640 insect eggs hidden in the cleavage of one brave woman's breasts. "There were many obstacles," Jan Hasnal says. "But I am so glad I did it."

A Total Solar Eclipse Showing the "Diamond Ring" Effect

ECLIPSE VIRGIN
THE BLACK SEA

My father decided it was time for my initiation. I was, after forty-plus years, still a virgin—an eclipse virgin.

Let me explain.

If you've never experienced a total solar eclipse, that's what you're called: an eclipse virgin. We're talking about that elegant astronomical collusion during which the earth, the new moon, and the sun are perfectly aligned. Partials don't count, and the moon doesn't either. It's a moment hung in time: a mere blink in the lifetime of our solar system—but oh, what a blink! People who experience it are invariably reduced to weak-kneed wonder. Some undergo an on-the-spot conversion from eclipse virgin to eclipse chaser.

For this particular celestial meetup we converged in Athens, boarded the sailing ship *Marco Polo*, and headed northeast through the Straits of Bosphorous and into the Black Sea. Most of the participants had already seen several eclipses. I couldn't help but wonder what brought them back for another and then another—and why some of our group were so excited they hardly slept the night before.

My father, an amateur astronomer, has witnessed five total solar eclipses in his seventy-eight years. He has lusted after glossy pictures of them in *Sky & Telescope* magazine, chased around the world after them, and photographed them. He even took me to see one. It was Wednesday, August 11, 1999: the final total solar eclipse of the last millennium—my first time.

Dad tried to describe the event before we went. "Everyone around you *ooohs* and *aaaahs* and screams, and then cries during totality," he explained. "It's a very emotional experience, like ... well, you'll see."

Then he decided to tell me the whole truth. In a halting voice, Dad explained that experiencing a total solar eclipse is "like being in the middle of a big group orgasm." Being an adult, and capable of some degree of discretion, I let the obvious question pass unasked. *What could my father possibly know about a "big group orgasm"?* Apparently, I was going to find out.

In order to *experience* totality, Dad explained, we had to be in the *path* of totality. *The Path of Totality*: It sounded like something a radical religious sect might insist its converts adhere to. And, indeed, it turned out that we were in the company of fervent seekers. Several hundred astronomers and their families, along with a former astronaut, a Nobel laureate, and the publisher of *Sky & Telescope* magazine, had traveled halfway around the world to witness this electrifying event.

The sky was clear, and the atmosphere bright with anticipation as our group crowded onto the *Marco Polo*'s wide deck after breakfast that day—hours before the event began—intent on adjusting our safety goggles, checking the sun's ascension, and carefully positioning our equipment: fat telescopes, oversized binoculars, and high-end video cameras, all fitted with dark filters so we could watch without ruining our retinas. Because an eclipse blocks only a portion of the sun's ultraviolet rays, we needed protective goggles for viewing. Totality, when the sun is completely blocked by the moon, is the only time you can look directly at that burning orb without danger of permanent damage to your vision.

Hooded cameras on tall tripods moved among us, Darth Vader-like, as veterans jockeyed for the best viewing spot. "This is excellent!" one astronomer shouted, checking his charts and GPS. "We're right in the middle of the path of totality!"

"We'd better be," a deep voice called out in response. "It's been on the schedule for four billion years. The least we can do is show up in the right place."

While we waited, the astronomers reminisced about past eclipses in the Galapagos or Alaska, Paraguay or Iran. They told stories of outwitting crowds and weather, of mountaintop observation posts, illegal border crossings, and ill-considered visa requests. No destination was too remote, it seemed, and no hardship

211

too difficult, when the promise of a total solar eclipse sang its sirens' song.

I was enjoying my chat with a veteran eclipse chaser until he suddenly burst out, "Hey; we've got a virgin over here!" He meant me.

"She'll get the full two minutes, twenty-three seconds," someone nearby chuckled.

All this fuss for an occurrence that lasts less than two and a half minutes? Extraordinary minutes, yes, but how good could it possibly be?

Actually, the eclipse lasted for several hours from start to finish. During the early stages, it was difficult to tell anything was happening. Then I focused my green goggles right at the sun, and was surprised to discover a small, dark "bite" missing. Gradually the bite grew larger, until the sun was just a slim crescent.

Shortly before totality, romantic sunset reds and oranges glowed for 360 degrees, all the way around the horizon. The sky turned steely gray, the air cooled; goosebumps emerged on my bare skin. Because our source of light had been reduced to a sliver, the world took on a pinhole-camera-like quality. Shadows sharpened, and my eyesight became so clear, it was as though I had superhuman powers.

Soon the much-anticipated "Diamond Ring Effect" began. It occurs just before totality, when the last little bit of sunlight peeks out from behind the last crater on the moon's surface, creating the impression of a gigantic diamond engagement ring in the heavens. The black circle of the moon's shadow is the "hole," and the "ring" is a slender circle of golden light around the shadow's circumference. Finally, a brilliant white "diamond"— at least two carats, maybe three—blazes for a few stunning seconds, then disappears.

Then totality: that extraordinary time during which the participating celestial bodies are perfectly aligned, and the moon's darkness obliterates the daylight. Totality was what we were all there for.

Quietly expectant, breathing almost as a single being, we watched and waited. Cameras clicked and whirred like locusts in a biblical plague. Then—at the moment of totality—the crowd jumped and whooped. Two minutes and twenty-three seconds was a lengthy period, allowing us plenty of time to admire the sensual patterns of what astronomers call the coronal discharge: delicate undulations of the sun's outer atmosphere, ionized and streaming out into the cosmos. Astronomers murmured, prayer-like, as they gazed upwards. Couples hugged. A man proposed marriage; his companion accepted. A few people even cried, just like Dad had said.

Me? Well, I threw off those safety goggles with wild abandon and looked straight at the sun. And then, with a shiver, I joined the cheering mob—couldn't help myself. I had become a convert to the Path of Totality.

And, in that moment, I understood humanity's age-old fascination with eclipses. They connect us with the heavens. We had not merely watched a total solar eclipse; we had *experienced* it. We had felt the miracle of a billion years, of a celestial clock timed to infinity, of darkness followed by resurrection. And, without fear of blindness, we had looked directly at the fiery orb that holds us in its gravitational pull and gives life to the earth, to each one of us, every day.

We had gazed upon the eye of God.

The Leaning Tower of Pisa,
with its Subtle yet Definite Banana-Shaped Curve

Banana Tower

PISA, ITALY

This was my father's rhyme:

> Paris has la Tour Eiffel
> Babylon had its tower as well
> But neither has the power to *seize ya*
> Like the Leaning Tower of Pisa

When I was young, he bounced me on his knee, reciting the words in a hushed and tuneless monotone. Every time he got to *seize ya*, he grabbed my shoulders and squeezed, and I shrieked in a confusion of fear and delight.

Dad taught high school physics and astronomy, and my bedtime stories often featured such heroes as Copernicus, Borelli and daVinci. And Galileo. How bold Galileo seemed, overturning Aristotle and challenging the Inquisition! How brilliant his mind, to invent the telescope, discover the moons of Jupiter, and develop elegant theories of periodic motion. How many times I imagined him standing at the top of that famous bell tower in Pisa, holding a cannon ball in one hand and a wooden ball in the other, poised to demonstrate the laws of gravitational acceleration.

Pisa infused my imagination for years: art, science, and religion, steeped through time, reappearing at occasional lucky moments in TV specials and history books, in art classes and in my dreams. It reminded me of my father, and of great men throughout history; in my young psyche, the city came to represent civilization itself. I longed to see the Santa Maria della Spina, a gorgeous, three-spired gothic church that houses a single thorn from Christ's crown. Christ's blood surely must have permeated that thorn, must have been part of it for more than 2,000 years, must still be part of it at this very moment. Campo Santo gave me the shivers: a graveyard containing dirt the Crusaders brought back from the Holy Land, filled with crumbling sarcophagi—some of which had been used over and over again. Imagine the jumble of DNA and dirt, memories and history, ghosts and skeletons there! And I wanted to visit the Arsenale, where the remains of more than fifteen ships are skeletons, too, their well-preserved ribs protruding unmistakably from ancient silt, recalling Pisa's glory days as a wealthy seaport.

More than anything, I wanted to climb the steps of the Leaning Tower of Pisa. The monument was built over the course of two hundred years, and the fact that the tower leaned was evident early-on. Architects attempted to rectify the situation by constructing the tower itself on a compensatory slant, and the result is a subtle but definite banana-shaped curve. As a child, I thought of it as the Banana Tower.

Many times I had imagined myself in Pisa, holding my father's hand, wandering intimate, arcaded streets, then strolling across the manicured Field of Miracles— a stately central lawn—toward a wildly tilting Banana Tower. I didn't know why the surrounding area was called the Field of Miracles, but supposed the Virgin had probably appeared to someone there. That, or an innocent baby had been cured of a horrible disease. Perhaps both, since it was called the Field of Miracles— plural. The sky radiated bright blue (it never rained in my imagination), the grass rolled out a perfect, verdant carpet (despite the lack of rain), and the bright sun reflecting off white marble nearly blinded me. The Banana Tower's cool, curved interior beckoned in welcome relief.

Escaping the heat of the day, I would enter a world of fantastic animals, with monsters and sea battles and hog-bears circling around me, no less frightening because they were captured in stone. Eight hundred years ago, children just like me had entered the tower and shuddered at the *animali mostruosi*—monstrous animals—then hurried up the steps to the comfort of plain limestone block walls, punctuated only by the sunlight streaming in at each narrow window. We climbed the tower many times, those children and I, all 294 steps. I still remember that odd hog-bear from one of my childhood picture books; I remember the serpents and the battleships sailing on wiggly waves as though I had seen them myself.

I had dreamed many times of visiting the Pisa of my childhood imagination, and now, twenty-three years later, I was climbing the stairs of the famous Leaning Tower. Even though I knew it would not look much like a banana, and would not be filled with the delicious banana aroma I had imagined as a child, I was still mildly disappointed.

There were only a few animal sculptures at the base of the monument, and they were smaller than I had expected. After I'd rounded the central column three times, I felt pleasantly off-kilter. But by the fifth, the combination of close quarters, physical exertion, a dizzying tilt, and pushing tourists conspired to make me reconsider my plan to reach the top. Not only were the stairs themselves slanted, they were also deeply worn—from the footsteps of millions of visitors during the past eight centuries—and maintaining my balance became increasingly difficult.

The alternating darkness and bright sunlight made my head ache, and I thought the view from the top of the tower was probably not as exhilarating as I had previously imagined. What sense was there in continuing, only to be disappointed? But the crowd behind me was insistent; it became a sinuous sea serpent, pushing me upward and devouring all hope of escape.

At the top, fresh air and an expansive view rejuvenated me. The Baptistery far below looked like a giant wedding cake, creamy white and layered and voluptuous, with its egg-like dome. The vast piazza was hemmed with an exuberant string of souvenir stalls, and beyond that stretched ochre-tiled rooftops, narrow streets, medieval palaces, and the winding Arno River.

Ah, the Arno. Wide and lazy, it is a placid reflectory for the noble palazzos lining its banks. Perhaps silk merchants had lived in these palaces, presiding over open-air markets here at the end of the exotic Silk Road, which once stretched all the way to China. Surely they strolled across the Ponte di Mezzo, enjoying the afternoon breeze and picnicking on salty olives and pungent pecorino.

I was beginning to imagine Galileo standing beside me—I would happily hold the cannon ball for him, my father would join us—and could have continued my medieval reverie indefinitely, but our guide indicated that the group must descend. Tours were tightly scheduled, and I had time for just one last look from the Leaning Tower. Tourists in the piazza below assumed the I'm-holding-up-the-tower pose—arms outstretched, one leg bent—for their companions with cameras. Cliché, but I couldn't help smiling along with them. Click. "OK, now *you* hold it up and I'll take the photo, then we've got to catch the bus." Click. A crowd was gathering for the next tour. Souvenir vendors hawked their wares: miniature towers, books and postcards, tea towels and salt-and-pepper sets, keychains, plastic skulls and lizards—reminders of the Campo Santo.

"*Andiamo!* Time to go!" Was this what Pisa had become? Tourists herded from one attraction to another, planning their day around the bus schedule, rushed into and out of the Leaning Tower, purchasing plastic mementos destined to gather dust on far-away bookshelves? My heart sank in bitter disappointment: Science and religion had abandoned this place. Romance, beauty and history had deserted; civilization had fled. Had it been this way for ten years, or for one hundred? Did my father know? Had he known all along?

I looked more closely.

A gray-haired couple, well-dressed and holding hands, emerged from the Duomo, admiring its intricate, multicolored stonework: mosaic stars, complex geometric patterns, long, calm bands of gray-green marble. Unhurried, they ambled towards the Baptistery, stopping to watch a flock of pigeons pecking at the grass.

Nearby, a woman about my age sat on a bench. Her face was flushed, and I thought her feet must be tired, because a pair of black, high-heeled sandals sat on the bench beside her. On the woman's lap was a small child, barely old enough to sit by itself, but already with a head full of the kind of fine blond hair that looks like cornsilk, and sparkles in the sunshine. I wondered whether this child, too, had heard stories of Galileo and Copernicus, of ancient sailors and the moons of Jupiter.

Slowly, the woman began to bounce her knees, and her child squealed in delight. I couldn't hear the woman's words, but I knew my father's rhyme by heart:

> Paris has la Tour Eiffel
> Babylon had its tower as well
> But neither has the power to *seize ya*
> Like the Leaning Tower of Pisa.

Afterword

and

Reading Group Guide

A Giraffe in Kenya

NATURE

Travel has allowed me to appreciate nature in a way that would be impossible at home. The African savannah, for example, is the best place in the world for viewing large, charismatic animals: lazing lions, grazing giraffe, zebras with their crazy stripes. And Madagascar is the only place in the world to see lemurs in their native habitat. Observing them in the wild is an awe-inspiring experience. Visiting Madagascar, Botswana, Costa Rica, and Queensland, Australia brought me into close contact with species I began to love and wanted to help protect.

And each trip brought up complicated questions...

Tracking lemurs in Madagascar got me thinking about the inherent conflict between humans and animals in a land where they each need space to spread out in order to feed themselves. What if the humans involved adopted agricultural methods that required fewer resources than slash-and-burn farming—would there be room enough for both humans and lemurs in the rainforest? Is it fair to ask humans to change their traditional way of life?

Do animals have any natural rights? If so, what are they, and how do they compare with humans' rights? What *are* "natural" rights, anyway, and from what authority do they arise?

Learning the story of Stravinsky's life raised questions for me about determinism: Is it the destiny of some—or all—species to become extinct? If so, do we have any responsibility to help keep them alive as long as possible? If we do, what does that say about the way we think about morality *vis a vis* time, and, by extension, about quality vs. quantity: Is a longer life better than a short one? What about an individual animal—in this case, a gorgeous little bird who was rescued from certain death in the wild? How do quality of life and length of life affect questions of environmental impact? How much can one individual really know about the quality of another's life?

In *The Truth about Eco-Travel* I learned, in a small and completely unexpected way, what it means to become one with the environment. Which raised the question of what it means *not* to be one with the environment....

Are human beings charged with being stewards of nature? If so, does that mean we are separate from nature—or can we be stewards of ourselves? If our way of life is in conflict with the survival of another species—or with our own grandchildren's future lifestyles—how do we think about the decisions we make?

What factors should we consider when we're thinking about habitat loss and extinction—basic human needs like food, space, timber, and economic growth? Human population growth? The potential benefit of medicines made from rainforest plants? Other benefits to humans that arise from biodiversity? What about the wellbeing of plants and animals, and the overall health of the earth?

Am I being irretrievably irresponsible when I fly in a fuel-guzzling jet to commune with an endangered species? Is there any way I can rationalize such far ranging travel? Should simply I stop going? Does it matter?

These questions do not have simple answers, but it is important to discuss them anyway: They are part of an essential global conversation that will benefit from our participation.

Balinese Dance Class

CULTURE

In many ways, people are *not* the same everywhere, and travel helps us to become more attentive to, and appreciative of, those differences.

In Kenya I learned about the Maasai's lifestyle. They are nomadic, own very few possessions, and measure their wealth in terms of cattle. (Actually, the part about measuring wealth in terms of cattle is not so different from American ranchers.) My "marriage" to a Maasai warrior was the result of my *faux pas* at the Maasai's show for tourists. (At least I *think* that's what was going on.) The incident made me consider the implications of being a guest in another culture: How much do I need to adjust my own way of being when I'm in a society that's very different from my own?

It also raised questions about the relationship between locals and tourists, and the complicated role tourism plays in economies. The Maasai village we visited, like many other places in the world, seemed to be economically dependent on tourism. That kind of dependence is apparently inevitable; it has been going on since traders traveled the Silk Route, at least. But it needs to be managed, and whose responsibility is that? We cannot freeze a place in time, so how should we think about the pros and cons of maintaining the integrity of our various cultures, many of which are already lost?

In *Searching for Sheela-na-Gig* I learned a little bit about how anthropologists decipher clues to the meaning of ancient relics. And I began to wonder how much of our "knowledge" about past cultures is subjective, subject to multiple interpretations, or perhaps the result of a perspective (that of a patriarchal social structure, for instance) that is not aligned with the culture under consideration.

I also explored the possible meaning of a controversial but almost-forgotten Celtic goddess. What was the real significance of the hairless, breastless, overtly sexual Sheela-na-Gig? Why don't we have any comparable present-day figures—or do we? How can incorporating the shadow side of life lead us toward wholeness?

Legends of Resistance recounts the clever ways in which southern Italians have responded to oppressive authoritarianism. Whether rebelling against the tax collector, the lord of the manor, or a Napoleonic decree, resilient Apulians have come up with delightfully inventive ways to circumvent unfair authority. These stories got me thinking about when it's right to break the rules—an especially important issue these days when whistle-blowers in America are being charged with espionage.

In fact, as news from around the world becomes a larger and larger part our daily lives, cultural literacy has become much more than an anthropological pleasure: It is a civic duty. Do I, as an outsider, have either a right or a responsibility to help stop the excruciatingly painful female circumcision that is common in Kenya, Egypt, and several other African countries? How would we feel if foreign nationals attempted to halt male circumcision in America? How would *they* feel about their attempt to end the cutting that does not, in the balance, confer any medical advantages?

Does the very fact of cultural diversity necessitate moral relativism? What are our responsibilities to our fellow human beings and what, if anything, is none of our business? I may not have the answers to these questions, but at the very least I can ask them, think about them, and discuss them with friends. And we can observe and celebrate cultural diversity together.

A Talented and Industrious Chef in Apulia, Italy

Cuisine

One of the most enjoyable ways of experiencing a culture is through its cuisine, which can illuminate quite a lot of history. Has the society been isolated, or have its people lived for centuries on a heavily traveled trade route? Has the food been influenced by people who have conquered —or been conquered by—the country? How have geography and climate affected the region's agriculture and cuisine?

In *Waist-ing Away in Apulia* I experienced gustatory ecstasy in the form of an exquisitely prepared fig, and willingly succumbed to mussel mania. Just as savoring those delightful morsels awakened my sensuality, the experiences in these stories awakened my thinking about food: What is food and what is *not food*—and why?

I can eat meat if I buy it in a store and don't think too much about where it came from, and if it's a fairly standard cut (no brains or kidneys, thank you very much). But eating food that is clearly the result of having slaughtered something is another story. No matter how delicious the blood sausage was in *An Irish*

Trinity, I could barely get it down because I was thinking about the reality of what it was—blood.

In *Could I Eat a Horse?* I tried to do just that, and discovered that the act is not as simple as it sounds. How different is a horse from a cow or a chicken, and why can some people eat one but not another? What if the horse was specifically raised for slaughter, like a hog? What if it was going to be shot anyway, because of a broken leg? Could I eat a pet? Would my answers be different if I were starving? Why? Is it wrong to be an omnivore—is veganism more moral (not to mention more ecologically efficient)? And what about plants— don't they supposedly "scream" when they are harvested? My only reliable course of action, when considering questions like this, is to embrace the age-old custom of reverence and thanksgiving for all food.

In *Magical Beans* I taste-tested luwak coffee, which is made from beans that have passed through the digestive tract of a small mammal and, obviously, come out the other end. Enzymes in the luwak's intestinal tract alter the chemistry of the resulting brew, converting it into something supposedly so delicious it has become the world's most expensive coffee. How much influence do stories like this have on the flavor—and our enjoyment—of food and drink?

I also learned, much later, that luwak coffee is made from the excrement of animals living in cages, possibly in crowded or otherwise inhumane conditions. That knowledge made the luwak coffee sample I'd carried home much less enjoyable.

As the world's population grows ... as weather extremes threaten crop stability ... as market manipulation increases food costs ... and as we begin to accept the fact that the successful Paleo diet of our ancestors included lots and lots of protein-laden insects ... we'll all need to re-think our ideas about food. I'm getting started now.

Incomprehensible Equipment at a Spa in Apulia

HEALING

From the simple—although sometimes confusing—pleasures of a steam bath to the more complicated processes involved in intuitive and indigenous practices, traveling has exposed me to many forms of healing.

In *Eat, Pray, Scrub* I sought out a Balinese healer, and was forced to confront my ideas about intuitive healing, trust, and common sense. The healer came with no particular recommendation, except that I had read about her in a best-selling book. She spoke only a little English, and I certainly did not speak Balinese. Her advice to the two Dutch girls before me smacked of charlatanism, as did her assessment of my health. (Bloat? Arthritis already showing? Really?)

So why did I swallow the pills she gave me? Are there any other circumstances under which I would take pills from strangers? Is there such a thing as a medical intuitive, and is Wayan one? How would I know—what evidence would I need in order to be convinced that Wayan's diagnoses were accurate, or that her treatments were effective?

Yerba Maté describes my experience learning about

South American herbal remedies from a wizened *curandera*, a handsome Argentine herbalist, and a Colombian botanist who teaches in New York City. The botanist is studying not only botanical cures, but also the relationship between health and "dis-ease" in traditional cultures. It's a sad irony that wisdom about traditional plant-based remedies is being lost as residents of remote South American forests increasingly adopt modern values.

Indigenous cultures tend to acknowledge the emotional aspects of healing more than American medicine does—and emotional healing was what I needed after my parents died. As I grieved, the whole of Paris conspired to haunt me until at last I gave in and allowed myself to be enveloped by a city that understands—and celebrates—death. Experiencing *Death in Paris* helped me begin the healing process. It also got me thinking about our society's approach to death, and wondering to what extent people in other cultures have different responses.

Who knows what we might gain by better understanding other cultures—and what knowledge and wisdom we might lose as remote cultures disappear, or are absorbed into larger, more aggressive, or more dominant ones?

A Rose Blooming in the Gardens at the Rodin Museum in Paris

GRATITUDE

Traveling offers endless opportunities for gratitude! In fact, the first travel story I wrote, *At a Crossroads*, was published in Lonely Planet's *The Kindness of Strangers*, an entire anthology of true tales about travelers who had been lost, confused, mugged, stranded, ill, mired in bureaucracy, or otherwise significantly inconvenienced ... and then helped out by a complete stranger. Reading it strengthens one's faith in the goodness of people all around the world.

I've been helped many times, and in many ways, while traveling. But it's important to be careful out there. I was very, very fortunate that my kidnapping in *At a Crossroads* turned out the way it did, and I am eternally grateful to the people who rescued me.

That is not the way abductions always turn out: I know a woman who was raped while hitchhiking, and a man who traveled—unaware—with a serial killer. By several estimates there are well over twenty million victims of human slave trade in the world today. I could have been one of them; thank God I was not.

In *Speaking Malagasy* I was reminded by a very poor

Malagasy girl of how much I have to be grateful for. A friend asked me, after reading the story, whether we need to be more fortunate than others in order to appreciate our blessings. Of course not! I can simply recall the children's prayer my grandmother taught me to be certain of that:

> Thank you for the world so sweet,
> Thank you for the food we eat.
> Thank you for the birds that sing,
> Thank you, God, for everything!

Yet, it *is* true that my friend had a point: We're more aware of our blessings when we are removed from the familiarity of our everyday circumstances, when we are reminded of conveniences we often take for granted, or are forced to struggle a bit in order to find our way around or make ourselves understood. New experiences keep our perceptions fresh. And that's another wonderful reason to keep traveling.

One of a Million Gorgeous Mountains in Southeast Alaska

INSPIRATION

We can find inspiration almost anywhere—in a poem, a place, a relationship, an event. But it's easier to become inspired in a new place because we are exposed to new circumstances—travel helps us experience life in a fresh way.

In *Silk from Ashes* I learned, up close, about some of the after-effects of war: pain, hunger, loneliness, displacement, fear, and humiliation. Jan Hasnal's actions were a huge inspiration for me. Would I have been as persistent as she was in locating silk worm eggs and bringing them into the country, or would I have been discouraged by early failures, or deterred by customs regulations? How do we decide when it is OK to break the law? I cannot even imagine what it's like to live in a war zone or, for that matter, in a crime-ridden neighborhood of Oakland, right across the bay from me. Hearing Hasnal's story opened me up to feel compassion where before I had felt no connection.

Astronomy has never been of particular interest to me, but in *Eclipse Virgin* I learned firsthand why solar eclipses have fascinated and inspired people for all of recorded history, why astronomers and amateurs alike feel compelled to chase eclipses around the world, why moments of totality and diamond rings and coronal discharges so excite the imagination: They expose us to the history of the whole of creation.

In *Banana Tower* I visited a centuries-old architectural icon, the Leaning Tower of Pisa, which had captured and held my imagination for years. Once there, I had to confront the reality of what the Leaning Tower has become: a tourist trap, complete with hurried travelers and pushy souvenir vendors. A seemingly insignificant event provided a moment of redemption, though, and I came away in love, once again, with the Banana Tower. I also came away with a deep and visceral understanding that love and acceptance do not depend on perfection.

Oddly—and wonderfully—that understanding has extended to my relationships with people. After visiting the Banana Tower I became more loving and accepting of the imperfections in my friends, my family, and myself. This is one the most important things we ask of travel—that it changes us for the better.

DISCUSSION QUESTIONS

1. Do animals have any natural rights? If so, what are they?

2. How much can one person really know about another's quality of life?

3. What are the pros and cons of celebrating cultural diversity?

4. How do we determine what our responsibilities to our fellow human beings are, and what is none of our business?

5. Are there any "foods" you would refuse to eat? Would you eat a pet if you were starving?

6. If a "medical" treatment only worked because of the placebo effect, would you recommend it to a close family member?

7. Are there any circumstances under which you think it's OK to break the law? Why? What are they?

8. Who has inspired you? Who have you inspired?

9. Do you need to be (at least a little) more fortunate than someone else in order to feel appreciative?

10. Have you ever been helped by a complete stranger?

ACKNOWLEDGEMENTS

PUBLICATION NOTES

ABOUT THE AUTHOR

Acknowlededgments

This is my first book, and I am grateful to the many people—way too many to name individually here— who have encouraged me over the years to write seriously.* You may not have realized the impact of your comments, congratulations, and appreciative laughter, but they inspired me to transform a few initial essays into a book with substance.

I received essential instruction and immeasurable support from the members of my various writing groups, especially the original Itinerants: Camille Cusumano, Bill Fink, Connie Hale, Gayle Keck, Laura Read, and Michael Shapiro; and from Larry Habegger, who published many of my essays in Travelers' Tales anthologies. Thanks, also, to Linda Watanabe McFerrin and Joanna Biggar at Wanderland Writers, who published nearly half the essays in this collection.

I especially appreciate Don George, the first editor to publish my work; Linda Watanabe McFerrin, who convinced me I could write well and then lovingly badgered

---

*It is my first book not counting *An Erotic Alphabet*, which was written under a pseudonym and was definitely not serious—it was barely even a book. But it still gets a lot of laughs.

me into doing so; and Kaye McKenzie, whose wise counsel guided me through the treacherous prepublication period.

My late parents, Jim and Pat King, are *so* represented in this book. Mom was a widely published poet and a disciplined philosopher who loved learning about other cultures. Dad—a scientist and teacher at heart—had a deep and curious mind. They both inspired my love of nature. And they both exposed me to the wider world with annual family camping vacations to national parks, and by hosting foreign exchange students and adults from other countries in our home. Thanks, Mom and Dad.

Finally, a huge thank-you to Jim, who has supported me in every way and without whom this book would never have been born.

PUBLICATION NOTES

Many of these essays, or similar versions of them, have previously been published elsewhere:

An Irish Trinity was published in *Venturing in Ireland: Quest for the Modern Celtic Soul* (Travelers' Tales, 2007).

At a Crossroads was published in *The Kindness of Strangers* (Lonely Planet, 2003).

Banana Tower was published in *30 Days in Italy: True Stories of Escape to the Good Life* (Travelers' Tales, 2006).

Bien-Être in the Hammam was published in *Wandering in Paris: Luminaries and Love in the City of Light* (Wanderland Writers, 2013). The anthology won first place in its category at the 2014 London Book Festival.

Big Cats, No Guns! was published in *The Best Women's Travel Writing 2009* (Travelers' Tales, 2009). It won a 2008 Travelers' Tales Solas Award for best "Animal Encounter" story, and a silver award in the Bay Area Travel Writers' 2010 International Planet Earth contest.

Could I Eat a Horse? was published in *Venturing in Italy: Travels in Puglia, Land Between Two Seas* (Travelers' Tales, 2008).

Death in Paris was published in *Wandering in Paris: Luminaries and Love in the City of Light* (Wanderland Writers, 2013). The anthology won first place in its category at the 2014 London Book Festival.

Eat, Pray, Scrub was published in *Wandering in Bali: A Tropical Paradise Discovered* (Wanderland Writers, 2012).

Eclipse Virgin won 2nd place in the 2013 Book Passage Travel Writers and Photographers Conference travel story contest.

French Kiss was published in *Wandering in Paris: Luminaries and Love in the City of Light* (Wanderland Writers, 2013). The anthology won first place in its category at the 2014 London Book Festival.

Keys to the Outback was published in *The Thong Also Rises* (Travelers' Tales, 2005).

Lemurs and Leeches was published in the *San Francisco Chronicle Magazine* in March, 2006. It won the grand prize in Bay Area Travel Writers' 2008 International Planet Earth contest, and appeared in *Animal Addict's Guide to Global Volunteer Travel* in 2011.

A version of *Lost* was published online as a Travelers' Tales Editors' choice story titled *Which Way is North?*

Magical Beans was published in *Wandering in Bali: A Tropical Paradise Discovered* (Wanderland Writers, 2012).

Searching for Sheela-na-Gig was published in *Venturing in Ireland: Quest for the Modern Celtic Soul* (Travelers' Tales, 2007).

A version of *Silk from Ashes* was published in *Travel Stories from Around the Globe* (Bay Area Travel Writers, 2012). The story won the Society of American Travel Writers' Lowell Thomas Gold Award in its category in 2013.

Stravinsky's Gift was published in *Wandering in Costa Rica: Landscapes Lost and Found* (Wanderland Writers, 2010).

The Truth about Eco-Travel won a travelers' Tales Solas award in 2008 for best "Bad Trip" story.

Waist-ing Away in Apulia was published in *Venturing in Italy: Travels in Puglia, Land Between Two Seas* (Travelers' Tales, 2008).

If you enjoyed these stories, I'd appreciate your
comments on IndieBound.org, Goodreads.com,
and/or wherever you purchased your book.
Thanks very much!
—Laurie

ABOUT THE AUTHOR

Laurie McAndish King grew up in rural Iowa, studied philosophy and science at Cornell College, and has traveled to nearly forty countries. She observes with an eye for natural science, and writes with a philosopher's heart and mind.

Laurie's award-winning travel essays and photography have appeared in many publications, including *Smithsonian* magazine, Travel Channel affiliate iExplore.com, Travelers' Tales' *The Best Women's Travel Writing*, and others. Her story *Silk from Ashes* won a Lowell Thomas gold award, and her mobile app about the San Francisco Waterfront earned a 5-star rating on iTunes.

Laurie also wrote *An Erotic Alphabet* (for which she was dubbed "The Shel Silverstien of Erotica") and co-edited two volumes in the *Hot Flashes: Sexy little stories & poems* series. She is an avid photographer—one of her photos was displayed at the Smithsonian Institution—and enjoys gardening, taxidermy, and chasing the cosmic serpent. Laurie lives in northern California with her husband and two cats.

Her website is www.LaurieMcAndishKing.com.

Made in the USA
San Bernardino, CA
21 July 2014